*One is never tired of painting because you have to set down*
*not what you knew already but what you have just discovered.*
*There is a continual creation out of nothing going on.*

# Easel in the Field

THE LIFE OF McINTOSH PATRICK

Ron Thompson

Culross

# Doctor James McIntosh Patrick

**OBE, RSA, ROI, ARE, LL.D, D.Arts**

PHOTOGRAPH · DEREK ROZE

# Easel in the Field

## THE LIFE OF McINTOSH PATRICK

Ron Thompson

WM CULROSS & SON LTD
2000

First Published 2000 by Culross

Produced and Published in Scotland by
Wm. Culross & Son Ltd.
Coupar Angus
Perthshire
Scotland PH13 9DF
Tel: 01828 627266
Fax: 01828 627146
Email: culross@btinternet.com

ISBN 1 873891 43 1

# Contents

# List of Illustrations – etchings, paintings, sketches, photographs

# *Introduction*

This book is not aimed at academia or at those
who inhabit the intellectual heights of the art establishment,
nor do the contents require the gloss of a recommendation by a famous name.
The work of James McIntosh Patrick speaks for itself.
There is certainly no attempt here to examine the man's inner soul
and then produce a litany of complicated reasons to explain why he became
the most popular landscape painter Scotland has yet produced.
Such forensic examination may be for others to undertake in the future.

This biography simply tells the story of how his paintings –
and his equally natural gift for teaching – so entranced a mass audience
and struck a chord with ordinary people
that he was crowned the "People's Artist."
We, therefore, offer this as a "People's Book."
McIntosh Patrick had no time for pretension or ostentation and never indulged in complex self-analysis.
He was a humble and modest man – but not unduly so.
Asked about art he would always say it should be *great fun.*
Asked about nature he would declare it a miracle which could never be copied by man.
Asked about life generally he would reply:
*Yes, isn't it wonderful? I simply can't get enough of it.*
And asked how he would wish to be remembered he said, almost diffidently:
*Oh, as a landscape painter, a Nature lover – someone who got great satisfaction
out of the bit of the world he was born into and never found anything better.*

It was once written:
"If being a landscape painter, it is the love of the hills and trees that move you,
then the spirit is upon you and the earth is yours and the fullness thereof."
These were not the words of James McIntosh Patrick.
But they could have been.

Ron Thompson
Dundee, May, 2000

# *Acknowledgements*

This book was not an easy one to put together, given the global distribution of the artist's work and the need to seek the permission of a widely-scattered ownership to reproduce his paintings and drawings. Tracking down transparencies and photographs was another time-consuming pursuit. In accomplishing these tasks, and for the generous assistance enjoyed in gathering background material, together with help in other ways, we wish to acknowledge our grateful thanks to a large number of individuals and organisations. They include: D C Thomson & Co Ltd; the Paladini family of Eduardo Alessandro Studios, Scottish Contemporary Art; The Fine Art Society Ltd; McManus Galleries of Dundee City Council and Clara Young, the Heritage Programme Officer; Robert Louden; Barbara Wishart; Douglas Phillips; Mr & Mrs Sandy Saddler; Roderick Fraser of Fraser & Son; Derek Roze; Bede Pounder; John Brown; Mr & Mrs Neil Livingstone; James Sinclair; Mrs Cathie Macfarlane; Peter Trowles at Glasgow School of Art; Roger Billcliffe for permitting use of extracts from his Exhibition catalogue introduction; Mr & Mrs Ken Borchardt; Irene Furlong; Joe McIntyre; Cynthia Thulbourne; Fred Livingstone; Derrick Edward; the Rt Hon Lord Macfarlane of Bearsden; the Very Rev Dr James L. Weatherhead; Ella Benzies; many national and city galleries throughout the world and, of course, Andrew Patrick and Ann Hunter, the son and daughter of McIntosh Patrick.

# Setting the Scene

I T IS THE summer of 1946 and Britain is getting back on its feet after the Second World War. Four artists are climbing into the back of a cab outside the Royal Academy in Piccadilly, London, where the annual exhibition has just opened. As they settle down they each tell the driver where they wish to go.

When it comes to the turn of the trim, studious-looking man with spectacles and thinning hair, not quite forty, he asks to be dropped off at King's Cross Station, explaining that he is catching the train back to Scotland. The others fall silent for several seconds as if their companion has just announced his own self-destruction. Then one exclaims: *Scotland! Surely you're not returning there?....No, no, no. You must send a telegram to your wife and tell her to join you in London. A person of your talent will do far better down here than up there in Scotland.*

The man from Dundee smiles at the prospect. *Perhaps you're right*, he concedes, speaking in a rich East coast accent which belongs a good bit north of Hadrian's Wall. Then, thoughtfully, adds: *But, you know, I think I would rather do less well in Scotland than do better in London.* And with that declaration of intent he turns to the driver once more and confirms his destination as King's Cross.

Later that day, as the Flying Scotsman pulls into Berwick-on-Tweed, James McIntosh Patrick glances out of the carriage window. Suddenly he spots a huge poster sliding into view on the station platform. It shows a glorious panorama of the gentle, rolling countryside of the Scottish Borders. He recognises the scene immediately. It is a print from his own painting commissioned by the London and North Eastern Railway Company. A look of contentment spreads across his lean, angular face. In a few more minutes he will be back in Scotland, and it is in Scotland that he will remain as an artist for the rest of his life.

W HEN Major James McIntosh Patrick had come marching home from war to his wife and two young children early in 1946, his kit bag was full, not with the usual souvenirs of battle, but with watercolour paintings and sketches he had completed during his off-duty hours in the North African and Italian campaigns.

This work was quite different to his epic landscapes of the 1930's, including the much-acclaimed **Four Seasons** and **Glencoe**, which had placed him firmly in the van of Scotland's most promising young painters. These, and his other oils, had been executed in a classical, rather formalised, tight style, reminiscent of the Old Masters. He had been proud to belong to the same profession as Rubens and Rembrandt. He still was. But now there was a difference.

**Patrick in 1946**   *DC Thomson & Co Ltd, Dundee*

The demands of war, serving not far behind the front line as a camouflage officer, had forced him to change his painting style. No longer had he been able as before to largely invent his landscapes in a studio, idealised compositions gloriously assembled from different sketches of the Scottish countryside. Now he had been compelled, through the lack of indoor facilities and the luxury of time, to work quickly on location with watercolour, capturing his scenes as they appeared before him "live". This had been the army Mr Patrick.

Working thus with a more relaxed brush out of doors, his style now owing more to the Impressionist school than the Renaissance, McIntosh Patrick would go on to enhance his reputation as a great landscape painter at a popular level never previously scaled by a Scottish artist, conquering a mass market in the new post-war, home-owning society where people were much more interested in having real paintings on their walls than plastic ducks above the fireplace.

This popularity enjoyed by Patrick would be earned through the dignified realism of his landscapes; charming portraits of domesticated rural settings, rather than the raw aspect of moor and mountain, which would circulate world-wide through the availability of reproductions on a high volume basis. This work would be found in galleries and public buildings, in castles and cottar houses, in royal palaces and private mansions, in bungalows and council dwellings. He was not without cause to become known as 'The People's Artist.'

AS THE post-war years passed quickly through the Fifties and Sixties, McIntosh Patrick would thus immortalise the Angus and Perthshire countryside within a 15-mile radius of his home in Dundee. The naturalism of his painting, in which one would almost feel and smell the country breezes wafting across the canvas, was to temporarily confuse many people into believing that he had actually created these vistas. Someone passing an attractive rural scene would often be heard to observe that it resembled 'a McIntosh Patrick,' as if he held the copyright of what rightfully belonged to Nature. Such exuberant admiration of his work which resulted in this role reversal was examined by William Blain, a fellow Dundonian and author of **Witch's Blood**, who, in contributing the introduction to the catalogue for the artist's first major retrospective exhibition in Dundee in 1967, wrote:

> Many of us never knew what it was to see the field patterns of Angus aright, to see a tree, a drystone dyke, a slated farm-steading, and newly-turned furrow, a corn stook, until his pictures had taught us to look. The architectural and engineering influences of his early days have given him an understanding of how mountains hold themselves together, the purpose of trees in the landscape, how fields are formed. Under his fields are a network of drains; they are fields in which farm folks work. His houses have rafters and beams behind the stones and slates; they are lived in. His furrows have been ploughed and sown upon.
>
> In time the scenes he has commented upon will have passed away. James McIntosh Patrick's pictures will be teaching men to look at what is past, as they once taught men to look at what was present. Objective though personal, documentary though poetical, his works will still have appreciation and purpose and effect. Honesty in the application of high skill, will then, as now, as always, be seen to be the best policy.

**Glamis Village 1940 in pre war style**   *Oil from the National Museums and Art Galleries on Merseyside (Lady Lever Art Gallery)*

4   *Setting the scene*

**Glamis Village April 1946 in post war style**   *Oil by kind permission of Robert Fleming Holdings Ltd, London/Bridgeman Art Library*

Twenty years later Patrick's continuing popularity was such that his next major retrospective, to mark his 80th birthday in 1987, attracted over 100,000 visitors at its venues in Dundee, Aberdeen, and Liverpool. These were cup final crowds paying homage to an artist who had a strike rate nothing short of phenomenal.

The artist himself was never to be carried away with his success. He abhorred pretension, always preferring an uncomplicated approach to his art and life generally, and had this to say about the world around him: *Some artists see Nature as gloomy and threatening. I don't. I've always thought Nature a tremendously dignified sort of show, not at all frivolous, but a happy kind of thing....If people walking about didn't just look at their fellow men, didn't just have as their sole concern human beings, the whole world and its beauty would give them greatly increased happiness, I think - if they could only learn to appreciate it. If you don't find the world beautiful, it's a grim business staying alive.*

He held that view until the day he died on April 7, 1998, at the age of 91.

McINTOSH PATRICK was a high profile person, both as a painter and an outstanding teacher; a charismatic character who was to raise an army of fans any top-class sportsman or pop star would be proud to call his own. He also had a great capacity for friendship and compassion, was always ready to guide the hand of the amateur painter, and was invariably a most agreeable and affable companion. He always held firm to his own style and method of painting, treating with amused indulgence those who dismissed his work as 'glorified photography.'

**Loch Creran,** *from a private collection*

Sometimes, however, he would give vent to his feelings. There was one famous occasion when a school teacher in England came across a framed painting in a load of junk his elderly neighbour was disposing of and, 'for a laugh,' took it along to the BBC's Antiques Roadshow where he ventured the opinion that the picture was 'amateurish' and not worth more than £50.

This, of course, was one of the popular features of the television programme, the failure of so many people to appreciate the value of their possessions.

In this case the painting was a McIntosh Patrick original, a sketch in oils of **Loch Creran**, between Oban and Appin, which had been painted forty years before and was now being valued by an expert at £6000. When the artist heard how the teacher had been so dismissive of his work before an audience of 15 million viewers he was far from happy. *The man doesn't know what he's talking about*, he retorted. *He should be more careful before passing such a judgement*. It was not surprising, therefore, given his extrovert nature, that a folklore would be created around the artist, a legend of anecdote and incident which would give him a personality status to enhance the wide and sustained coverage he was to enjoy in all branches of the media.

Following his war service he would spend almost every day on location, communing with nature in weather fine and foul. On one occasion when painting a farm scene he decided to open a barn door to achieve a more pleasing composition. In doing so a calf escaped and ran off, with Patrick in hot pursuit. Unable to recapture the animal, he summoned the assistance of the farmer and together they eventually returned the calf to its quarters. The artist was duly apologetic and as a gesture of reconciliation promised the farmer that he would include him in the picture, at work in front of the barn. But back in his studio later that evening he decided that the farmer didn't quite fit into the picture of things after all – so he duly painted him out. As he did so he turned to a friend watching him work, and said with a twinkle in his eye: *Now, for goodness sake never tell this man that I evicted him from his own farm!*

That remark typified McIntosh Patrick. To him, art was always great fun. It was also what he lived for. Painting had the same priority for him as football did for the famous Liverpool manager Bill Shankly who, when asked if he considered football to be a matter of life or death, famously replied: *No, I don't. It's much more important than that.*

# Growing Up

ALMOST all children at a very young age like to draw pictures of the familiar objects they find around them. Child psychologists will tell you that such activity signals the first stirrings of the creative spirit. James Patrick was no different in this sense to all the other infant artists...except in this way: from the very start his drawings were not mere scribbles evoking exaggerated gasps of delight from parents and fond relatives. His efforts with pencil and crayon had shape and form and bore more than a passing resemblance to that which caught his eye.

By the time he went off to primary school in Downfield, Dundee, at the age of five in 1912, it was becoming fairly obvious that his artistic talent was greater than most. This was hardly surprising considering the family history in this field. His father Andrew, who was an architect with a city practice, also painted in watercolour to a professional standard. His mother, Jean, was a pattern designer for damask tablecloths produced by a firm in Perth. His grandfather made model ships good enough to have become museum exhibits. In fact, the creative gene could be traced back through the family tree to the start of the 19th century.

James's first teacher quickly spotted his skill with paper and pencil and gave his bright little pupil pictures to copy and simple, illustrated books on art which he could study. He was also greatly encouraged at home and as he got older would often go off with his father on painting expeditions out of doors. At other times he could be found in his father's office drawing

*James painting as a young man in the country with mother and father*

impressions of the various architectural projects his firm were working on. During the first world war he and his pals staged concerts for various charities, with James painting the colourful sets. He appeared to have had a constant urge to express himself. This would even surface on the way to school in the mornings when he would call for a friend who lived in a block of flats. While waiting on his pal finishing his breakfast, James would draw crayon pictures on the

**A boyhood watercolour** *gifted to Sandy Saddler*

walls of the building, much to the annoyance of his friend's mother who always had the task of washing them off later.

As the Kaiser's war drew to a finish James moved on to secondary school at Morgan Academy where art enjoyed a high profile under its principal teacher James "Curly" Watson. He, too, coached his talented new pupil, instructing him in oils and providing much encouragement for his rapid advancement, although by now James could see the way ahead with his own style and subject matter. He never had to experiment in finding his metier. Even at that age he was his own man when it came to art. He was enthralled by Nature, and the beauty of the country-side was already filling the pages of his sketch books.

It was then, however, at the age of 14, that James was introduced to a different, and highly specialised, form of art which was to have a significant impact on his future career. This was etching. He was influenced in this by a friend of his father, CGL Phillips, a well-known Dundee artist who was an enthusiastic print maker. Etching is a method of making prints from a copper plate covered with an acid-resistant ground on which a design is drawn with a needle. When the drawing is completed, and the plate is placed in a bath of nitric acid, the exposed lines are eaten away. These recessed lines of the drawing retain ink and this imprint is transferred to paper by passing the plate through a flat bed roller. In order to reproduce a picture this way the etching of the subject must be done backwards as a mirror image to achieve a print showing the subject the right way round. This is particularly important if lettering is involved.

James was certainly fascinated by this form of drawing and was largely self-taught. Etching is a slow, meticulous process calling for great patience, fine draughtsmanship, and a technical ability greater than required in normal drawing. But the young schoolboy already possessed these attributes. He also had a natural eye for the close work involved with the plates, although in his early school days his eye-sight had caused certain concern. Unable to see writing on the blackboard from his desk at the back of the class, he was gradually moved forward until, at the very front, he was getting a clear picture. Spectacles then corrected this imbalance, but his short-sightedness gave him an added advantage at etching. By removing his glasses he gained a slight magnification and was able to work in fine detail which most people couldn't achieve without a magnifying glass. Soon James was producing impressive plates, running off his prints in the early stages on his mother's clothes mangle, known in Dundee as a wringer.

Despite his ever-increasing involvement with art, James always found time for a wide range of adolescent pursuits which included dancing, cricket, piano lessons and girl friends. He also became a boy scout whose shirt bristled with badges. There were even lighter moments with his art when he taught himself to draw and paint with both hands at the same time, a skill which his teacher would sometimes ask him to demonstrate on the blackboard for his classmates. This ambidexterity would come in useful much later when working outside in the winter, enabling him to transfer the brush to his other hand when his natural left hand was turning numb with the cold. He could also sign his name backwards at great speed, perhaps as a result of reverse drawing in etching, then hold it up to a mirror before an admiring audience to have his signature read the right way round. These diversions, of course, were little more than party pieces, but they revealed a sense of fun which was going to colour his attitude to art for the rest of his life.

THERE had never been any doubt that James would make art his career. From his first batch of drawing paper and box of paints it was clearly obvious he was born to be an artist. There is no evidence that he ever indulged in the popular boyhood fantasies of wanting to become an engine driver, a fireman, or a dustman. The artistic instinct was dominant within him. He couldn't escape. He was drawn to art with all the force of a small pin being sucked towards a powerful magnet.

His mother had voiced the opinion, in a somewhat light-hearted vein, that two architects in the family were more than enough, James's brother, William, twelve years his senior, having already followed his father into that profession. But James knew himself it was at the easel rather than the design board that his future lay, so there was no conflict on that score. Nor was there any doubt over the college he would attend to gain his qualification. At that time Dundee College of Art could award only a diploma course in design and not in painting, and as painting was to be an essential component of his armoury his gaze was firmly fixed on the more distant horizon of Glasgow School of Art. But apart from offering a curriculum more compatible to his needs, the Glasgow school had produced a famous crop of painters whom James admired, so it was to that nursery in the west of Scotland that he applied for a student place.

On the day of his interview James and his father caught the train to Glasgow, the young Patrick taking with him a portfolio of work required by the assessors. This contained samples of etchings, drawings, watercolours and oils. It was by any standard an impressive canon and one which convinced the assessors that this promising prospect from the east should not only be enrolled in the four-year diploma course, but should move immediately into the second year. This was a considerable achievement and was the first official signpost to a future of high expectation.

James was 17, and already possessed his school's medal for art, when he started his studies at the famous building in Renfrew Street, designed by the brilliant Scots architect Charles Rennie Mackintosh. The bouncy young man from Dundee slipped easily into student life and quickly pulled his chair up to the table in the digs which he and his father had chosen during their earlier visit to the city. The year was 1924, and although there was much unemployment and hardship there were also signs of a certain gaiety returning to life following the ravages of the First World War. James revelled in the atmosphere of freedom and the bonhomie which went with college life; the parties and the innocent high jinks of young men and women asserting themselves away from home. But the social calendar was never going to dominate his life. The main purpose of his existence was art and in many respects he was the perfect student, displaying a diligence and industry which produced work of high quality and at a frequency that impressed his lecturers.

He was rewarded for all this by being allocated a studio of his own in his second year, a rare occurrence indeed, and by the following year was appointed the monitor of the etching room. Etching had become his specialist subject and the fine detail and definitive draughtsmanship which he brought to his plates

*Glasgow School of Art*

conveyed more than a hint of his family's architectural background. At this time etching was carving a name for itself in the art market at home and abroad with prints by the acknowledged masters fetching hundreds of pounds. It was not entirely the thought of financial gain, however, that determined James to make his mark as an expert in this exacting medium. He simply wanted to excel.

This opportunity of establishing himself at a higher level arrived on two fronts in 1926, after he had been at the school of art for two years. First, he had work accepted for hanging at the annual exhibition of the Royal Scottish Academy - the etching, The Canal, Bruges - which was quite an accomplishment for someone still in his teens. Then he was able to undertake a drawing and painting expedition to Provence in the South of France.

*Opposite:* **The Canal, Bruges** *Private Collection*

**Roman Arena, Nimes**/*Christies Images Ltd*

This latter project was unexpectedly financed by the political events of the day created by the General Strike. In May that year the TUC (Trades Union Council) called out its members in a national stoppage of work in support of the miners who had refused to accept a cut in wages. The strike extended to all major industries, including all forms of transport, and in order to keep essential services moving non-union labour was drafted in. Work then became available at Glasgow Docks and James, along with many other students, seized the opportunity of earning a wage during the vacation. The work was of the toiling variety and sometimes lasted 18 hours a day, but by the end of his labouring stint James took off to the Continent with enough cash to see him through for three months on foreign soil.

That turned out to be a wonderful summer for the aspirations of the Dundee student as he moved from one Provencal town to another in glorious weather; Avignon, Nimes, Les Baux, Carcassonne, and several other centres. It seemed that everywhere he went the farms and buildings and streets had a picturesque quality which transferred to canvas and sketch book with a willingness and sparkle not so readily available at other locations. These months in France also had their moments of high drama.

James and other students from Scotland had arranged to meet up at the end of their stay and travel home together. Before having a final meal at their departure point they decided to deposit their luggage at the local railway station from where they would be catching the train north to Paris. When the station porter attempted to charge them for each item separately the Scots, with native ingenuity, tied all their bags and cases together to make one huge item, much to the annoyance of the official who reluctantly issued only a single ticket. James unfortunately lost the receipt and when the party returned to the station later the place looked deserted. Spotting the key in the door of the left luggage room, the students removed their belongings - then promptly walked into the arms of the porter whom they had earlier upset over his pricing policy. He immediately marched them off to the stationmaster who accused the students of theft and proceeded to note down the details in their passports. Things looked black. One student asked if he could 'phone his solicitor in Glasgow. The request was refused. Then, just when it seemed they might end up in the French Foreign Legion, the station-master relented and allowed the young artists to board their train.

The journey which followed was a nightmare. The train's lighting system failed and the compartments were crammed with troops and wounded soldiers returning from colonial strife in North Africa. The train stopped at every station and took more than 18 hours to reach the capital. Little did James know that sixteen years on he, too, would be in uniform in North Africa, fighting on the same side as the French in a different sort of war altogether.

BACK in Scotland with a portfolio bulging with the fruits of his Continental travels, James set about the task of capitalising on his labours. A Dundee collector bought six of his watercolours and he very quickly produced a set of etchings from the drawings he had completed in the south of France. When he took these prints to a local dealer for framing the man was so impressed by the precision and detail of the subjects that he suggested they be shown to two of the best known publishers in London, Colnaghi and Harold Dickens.

When James did this, Colnaghi asked him by letter to send down his next ten plates as he completed them with a view to publication. Dickens, however, adopted a more personal approach, inviting the young student to come and see him in London. This meeting resulted in Dickens agreeing to publish two of his plates right away and offering him a contract worth £200 a year for future work. This represented a fortune for James, still at Glasgow School of Art but now with an assured income from his etching. Such commercial success was a rare occurrence for a student, and with the comfort of a cheque book in his pocket he splashed out on a car.

This was no banger, but an almost new Cloverleaf Renault costing £75, a real sporty, soft-topped number half-decked over at the rear with polished teak lids. He bought it from a Dundee taxi firm whose owner drove the vehicle, with James as passenger, down to the Tay Ferry terminal. At that point they changed seats, and with young Patrick now at the wheel they drove a mile along the river front and back into the city. It was the only driving lesson James ever had.

The following day, with two friends aboard, he drove the 80 miles back to the art school in Glasgow. All was well until he found himself in the wrong lane at one of the city's busiest junctions. To make matters worse the engine stalled. At that moment a policeman on points duty brought all traffic to a halt, including several tramcars, and sauntered over to the stranded vehicle. After making a few sarcastic remarks about the driver's shortcomings behind the wheel, and with the engine now restarted, he escorted the car slowly across the junction and on its way. Needless to say the Cloverleaf Renault caused quite a sensation at the school. In these days student transport rarely took the form of the internal combustion engine. Nowadays you can't get moving for their jalopies.

These were certainly carefree years at the art school with a busy social calendar despite the hard grind of study and work. At that time the ukulele and the banjo were the popular musical instruments and James, whose proficiency at the piano was already quite considerable, would often strum away at parties with renditions of *Dinah, Ukulele Lady, Crazy Words,* and *Ain't Got a Barrel of Money*. The Charleston was also all the rage and the students would often dance it in the corridors between classes as a rehearsal for weekend gigs.

In the summer of 1927 James was awarded his Diploma of Art along with a post-graduate scholarship for a year. This bursary carried a maintenance grant to cover living expenses, but he later repaid this with the money earned from his etching contract, a gesture which was duly announced at the annual prize-giving ceremony at his old school, Morgan Academy, where James's fortunes were being followed with some pride. When he finally left Glasgow Art School in 1928 he took with him a clutch of prizes in etching, portraiture, and landscape painting, along with the James McBey Prize for Etching awarded by the Scottish Print Club. By then his work was becoming well known in the highest circles. Not only had he been hung on the line at the Royal Scottish Academy but, at only 21, was being exhibited at the Royal Academy in London.

His student years had been outstandingly successful and he had upheld the highest traditions of the school, achievements which no doubt were in the thoughts of Sir George Clausen who, in presenting his Assessor's Report of 1927, said: *The school has at present two or three students of quite remarkable promise whose compositions would give distinction to any school.* Sixty-seven years later, towards the end of his distinguished career, James would return to the striking art nouveau building in Renfrew Street to be given an Honorary Fellowship of Glasgow School of Art. On that occasion he would be wreathed in laurels, although tributes to his skills were already being acknowledged in professional journals as he waved goodbye to life as a student.

In the Apollo magazine of July, 1928, Malcolm Salaman described the young Dundee artist as an etcher who had "already attracted the notice of collectors by the completeness of his design and the precision of his linear scheme". He then singled out the print **Les Ramparts, Les Baux,** from one of the plates arising from Patrick's sojourn in the south of France, an etching considered by James himself to be the finest he ever did. Les Baux is a small mountain town built behind a rocky precipice. Salaman continued in his special article:

# An Etcher of Genius

## THE SCOTTISH LANDSCAPES OF J. MACINTOSH PATRICK

By a Special Correspondent.

MR J. MACINTOSH PATRICK is one of the most distinguished young artists in Scotland. As painter and etcher, he holds a high position among those artists still in their twenties who are beginning to win popular attention.

It is as an etcher Mr Patrick is chiefly known to collectors. His first etched plate was done when he was a schoolboy—his father is an architect and he inherited a love of drawing—and at the Glasgow School of Art, where he took his diploma, he was looked on as an etcher of most brilliant promise.

Mr Max Judge, in the current issue of the Print Collectors' Quarterly, does not hesitate to refer to him as an etcher of genius. Although it is not ten years since he made his first print, his total output is already more than a little impressive, and in the past two or three years his work has taken on a significance that there is no gainsaying.

* * * *

But although Mr Patrick's etchings, some of which are in American collections and two or three of which are to be seen in the British Museum, brought him his first and widespread success, his painting has also of late been attracting considerable attention.

*Mr J. Macintosh Patrick.*

the Glasgow Institute and elsewhere his painted landscapes have more than held their own with some of the best works on the walls.

At such exhibitions Mr Patrick occupies an enviable position—he has assimilated many of the most profitable lessons of the modernist movement without having to abandon that measure of tradi-

robes—but it is as a landscape painter he is chiefly represented in the present exhibition of the Dundee Art Society, and as a Scottish landscape painter he will perhaps ultimately be best known.

* * * *

Though he has worked abroad, in Provence and Belgium, the bulk of his work has been done in the Highlands.

Ever so many painters have hiked easels and canvas into the Highlands since Landseer painted those stags and misty glens for his Queen, and one count the really good pictures that resulted on one's fingers. Most Scottish artists knowing this, have saken this country for France, have come the most vital of art influences. Mr Patrick, stayed at home and worked to do for Highland land artist of, say, the calibre has done for English sc

In my own opinion, achieving the perfect such scenes as are to Ross-shire mounta Scottish or Englis the job. . . . Ir Mr Patrick a sense of the te he was traine

**Les Ramparts, Les Baux** *The Artist's Family*

In Les Ramparts, Les Baux, he gives us a well-planned conception of the ancient place, reaching away to the distant hills, constructing as he goes the rock-bound bastions, and the mean houses perched upon them, and further away the steep cliff towers and battlements in wonderful lordly ruin, with the poor town hiding behind and below, and intermediately the rocky and verdant places of the plain. The effect of the glaring light on the ramparts and the houses of the foreground, and the paler light on the farthest hills with all the multitudinous detail of the scene between in various gradations of shadow, makes a plate of distinctive interest.

Two years later, with Scottish landscapes having by then been added to the French subjects in a constant stream of prints from new plates, James was being hailed as a brilliant etcher. Certainly, few leaving the school in that summer of 1928 faced a brighter future than the young Dundee man as he prepared to take on the world with his artistic flair. Most graduates would go into teaching or become employed by firms engaged in various fields of commercial art. James was offered a teaching post in Paisley. But going from art school straight back into the classroom as a full-time occupation was not for him. He wanted to earn his living by the easel and the etching plate and he wanted to do it back in the city of his birth with the callour breezes of the East coast upon his face. Dundee was the city of jute, jam, and journalism. He was determined to play his part in putting it even more firmly on the map as a centre of artistic excellence as well.

## Early Career

WHEN James returned to Dundee in the summer of 1928 to put up his plate as a self-employed artist he could hardly have chosen a more difficult economic period in which to go it alone. Although the global Depression was not really to start until 1930, severe economic decline in Britain had already set in – indeed Britain had never recovered from the First World War – and with millions already out of work the Wall Street crash in America on October 29, 1929, ended any hope of an early recovery.

In such a climate luxury items are obviously first to feel the pinch and quickly become unaffordable. Art work clearly fell into this category at that time. Galleries were going to the wall and many gallery owners were being driven to suicide. With the etching market in a state of collapse one of James's main sources of income had almost dried up completely, although his eminence in this field would be recognised later when a number of his prints were purchased by the British Museum Print Room and others included in a programme of foreign exhibitions called British Graphic Art organised by the Department of Overseas Trade. This was rather like being 'capped' for your country and his 'performances' brought him favourable reviews from both America and Europe. In 1932 he was elected an Associate of the Royal Society of Painter-Etchers and Engravers and three years later, at the request of the Print Collectors' Club, he produced a plate, Kyleakin, for presentation to club members.

But these honours were still to come. In the dying months of the 1920's James needed work – and he needed it quickly. The publisher of his etchings had suggested that perhaps he should seek a different source of income. To which the artist replied rather tartly that since he couldn't do anything better than drawing and painting it was unlikely he could make a living doing something else. At that point several opportunities came his way. Dundee College of Art decided to offer a diploma in painting and, having just taken that qualification in Glasgow, James was invited to join the staff on a part-time basis teaching two mornings a week. Then the Dundee Courier, published daily by DC Thomson & Co Ltd commissioned him to pen a series of drawings of local landmarks with accompanying text. These ran every Saturday for eighteen months and proved to be a most popular series. Here again the drawing skills developed as a schoolboy in his father's architectural practice stood him in good stead and would form the groundwork of everything he would ever do. Indeed, he would later come to regard painting as simply drawing with colour.

## COUPAR ANGUS LANDMARK : Specially Drawn By J. M'Intosh Patrick

Coupar Angus is a town of remote antiquity.
A Roman camp, supposed to have been formed
either by Agricola or Lollius Urbicus, was situated
here. It appears to have been a square of 1200 feet,
with two strong ramparts and wide ditches.
In 1164 King Malcolm the maiden founded the
Cistercian Abbey of St. Mary's
within the area of this Roman camp.
Only a small fragment of this once stately pile
remains, a beautiful arch having been demolished in
1780 to furnish material to build the parish church.
This ivy-clad fragment is almost opposite
the tower in the drawing.
St. Mary's was richly endowed by several Scottish
Kings, and the Abbey flourished until the
Reformation, when, like similar buildings, it
suffered at the hands of the Reformers.
In 1618 the spirituality of the benefice was
transferred to the Protestant minister,
and a new church was erected.
In 1645, two hundred soldiers, by order of the
Marquis of Montrose, attacked the town, and
Robert Lindsay, the parish minister, undertook the
leadership of the defence, but at the cost of his life.
The steeple, which is familiar landmark to all who
travel the Dundee-Blairgowrie Road, is not
connected with the church. It was built in 1762 by
public subscription, and stands on the spot where
the Court of Regality stood.

*By kind permission of DC Thomson & Co Ltd, Dundee*

*An example of early draughtsmanship and journalism which brought
in a welcome income to the artist (see p 19).*
*Drawn in Queen Street, the building in shadow behind the steeple
became the offices in 1938 of the publishers Wm. Culross & Son Ltd.*

*The Tay Bridge*

Further work came from Valentines, at that time a leading British publisher of greetings cards and picture postcards based in Dundee. They, too, wanted him to produce a series of views, but this time to cover the whole of Britain. Working from photographs, James turned out dozens of drawings which were retailed nationally through Woolworths for many years under the trade name of Etchographs. Add to this another part-time teaching post at Trinity College, Glenalmond, a private school in Perthshire, and James had the basis of a regular, if somewhat modest, income. But these were all bits and bobs, and with etching no longer his mainstay he now turned to painting on a grand scale as a means of consolidating his future.

IN 1930 James had gone on a three-month working trip to Italy. Mussolini had already established a dictatorship in that country and introduced the infamous Blackshirts, the colloquial name for the Fasci di Combattimento which formed the backbone of Italian fascism. Although not greatly alarmed by their presence, James was conscious as a visitor of being eyed suspiciously by these ominously-uniformed thugs as he travelled about in trains and buses. But his discomfiture was soon overtaken by a sense of awe at the magnificent galleries of Florence and the impressive architecture of the many towns and cities he visited.

As an artist, however, looking for subjects to paint, it was Assisi that captured his imagination. This town in the central Umbrian region is the birthplace of St.Francis, who founded the Franciscan Order in 1209, and has two outstanding Gothic churches. In a letter home he wrote: *This whole place is so paintable I cannot bear to move on.* He stayed for two months, totally absorbed by the vistas and buildings offered by this charming hill town, producing paintings and sketches under clear blue skies which he could work up later back in Dundee.

There was one interesting distraction during his spell in Assisi. In the pension where he was staying he met a fascinating couple, an Englishman and his Italian wife who insisted on speaking to each other only in French. They had travelled all over Europe, living in different countries until they were due to pay taxes then dodging over the border to take up residence under a different flag. In one of the Slav countries the woman had bought a national bridal costume, a magnificently embroidered piece of work which enhanced her lovely figure and matched her black hair. James painted her portrait on a balcony with the Umbrian landscape behind. When shown later at an exhibition of the Society of Scottish Artists, **Slav Bride,** caused much admiring comment and sold quickly. Since then this striking picture has never resurfaced and James never set eyes on the couple again.

Returning to Dundee, James got down to the task of developing his skills as a painter. This, he now instinctively believed, was where his future lay. Establishing himself as such, however, was going to be no easy task and he suffered an early setback when his large-scale oil, **The Church of St. Francis, Assisi,** although exhibited at the Royal Academy in 1931, couldn't find a buyer. Painted from a high elevation, it showed the basilica dominating the landscape, almost like a fortress, with a vast plain merging into a distant range of hills. Several critics saw the work as a metaphor for the influence of the church beyond its own parish. But as far as the artist was concerned he had simply painted a noble building from an interesting position, displaying an uncanny sense of scale and perspective which was to distinguish all his future landscape paintings. One reviewer declared that his Assisi composition *has given sufficient proof of talent and inspiration to entitle him to claim a high place in British art.* However, despite being well received and much talked about, the canvas finished up back in Dundee.

This was certainly a set-back, financially and professionally, for someone who had been feted as a student but was now finding the going rather tough.

**St Francis, Assisi**  1935  *Oil 30 x 40 by kind permission of the South African National Gallery*

**The Rt Rev Monsignor Canon Turner** 1932 *Oil 44 x 30*
*Dundee Arts and Heritage, McManus Gallery*

Then he had a lucky break. It was almost an act of divine intervention given that he was commissioned to paint the portrait of a local Roman Catholic prelate, **The Right Rev. Monsignor Canon Turner.** The priest sat in his full robes, an impressive figure in a white lace-trimmed surplice under a magenta-edged cloak. Such a subject was a gift for an artist anxious to display his wares and James proceeded to produce a stunning portrait of detail, design and vivid colour which proved beyond all doubt that here was an artist, struggling perhaps to find a new niche, but one of enormous talent. This feat of skill also demonstrated his ability to paint in the same meticulous detail as he had shown in his etchings.

Over the years he would paint many other prominent figures, although, interestingly, never a study of himself. These portraits were highly regarded for presentation and likeness. Many critics claimed that he had the rare ability to bring out his sitter's finer qualities, capturing their inner strengths in the expression he achieved on the canvas. But James denied such extra-sensory perception, in the same way as he had rebuffed a more intellectual meaning for his Assisi composition. He would always shun complex theories about his work and have no truck with dilettantes. He was a cultured man in a very uncomplicated way, simply painting what he saw, but with an eye gifted with an observant quality not given to many others.

He could undoubtedly have become a fine portrait painter had he wished to follow that path. People enjoyed sitting for him. They felt at ease in his company. He was a good conversationalist and would speak as he worked, often alerting his subject to that part of their anatomy he was painting at any given time, thus allowing them to relax in those areas away from his brush. The Canon Turner picture had certainly boosted his cash flow. But, even more importantly, it had manifested beyond all doubt a technical brilliance and mastery of detail which was to shape his painting style in the years to come. It was, however, in the great outdoors that he now wished to deploy these skills.

More than anything he yearned to become a landscape painter. To say he was in love with the countryside, that great canvas of Nature's gifts, is to incline towards the facile. His feelings in this matter were almost spiritual, revealing a closeness to his Creator which, although never to be formalised in a religious sense, was always to be to the fore in his attitude to life. Many years later he would say: *I don't think you can really be a landscape painter in the true sense of the word unless the landscape is very meaningful to you. If you don't find this beautiful then you are that amount poorer in what you can get out of being alive.*

At that point in 1932 he turned his attention to a truly towering subject, to that great brooding, famous glen in the Highlands of Scotland which exudes an overpowering, domineering presence and melancholic air: Glencoe, the scene of treachery in 1692 when the Macdonalds were massacred by the Campbells, an infamous page of Scottish history which is still spoken of in many lands. He decided to capture its trio of peaks, known as the Three Sisters, in a winter setting. This was to be an epic picture. James himself later described it as "heroic". It would possibly be, even at this early stage of his career, the most ambitious project he would ever tackle, what could be described as a seminal work. Certainly he would never again spend two years over the same canvas. It was a tour de force that would cause him many anxious moments.

Month after month, using an earlier etching as his principal reference, he strove to create a dramatic effect with the use of silver grey tones, layers of paint scrubbed down to suggest a shimmering winter light filtering through thin cloud. He worked the picture over time and again, at one stage removing several months of work, in his effort to convey the eeriness of Glencoe as a gypsy family and their horse-drawn caravan, tiny figures against the massif, wended their way through the winding Pass. There were, of course, some lighter moments on location, like the day he found himself without cigarettes. Going into a wee shoppie he mentioned to the Highland lady behind the counter that he was a painter. *A painter?*, she said, eying him suspiciously. *But hoo can ye be a painter? There's nae hooses aboot here.* This case of mistaken identity was similar to the time in Fife when he asked someone to sit in for a picture. *You a painter?*, challenged the man. *I thought you looked mair like a grocer.* Then, noticing the look of bewilderment on the artist's face, quickly added: *Aye, but a licenced grocer, ye ken.*

It was, however, no laughing matter when the picture, finally submitted to the Royal Academy in 1934, was rejected by the selection committee. At that point a bitterly disappointed James contacted Harold Dickens in London who, following on the etching contract, was now acting as his general agent. He asked him not to send the canvas back to Dundee. What happened next is best described in the artist's own words: *I asked Dickens to keep it in London because I was terrified that if it came back to Dundee I would start to rework it. I had wiped out the **Assisi** picture and **Glencoe** had taken me the best part of two years and I couldn't face going through all that again. Anyway, Dickens kept it for a few months and then the new road through Glencoe was opened and it was in all the newspapers and Dickens suddenly realised that he had a topical picture on his hands. My picture was of the* *old road, when you set out in the morning and hoped to get to the top by the end of the day if the weather didn't change; and all of a sudden everyone wanted to know.*

*Dickens took it along to the Fine Art Society in Bond Street and they were amazed by it and put it in the window. I didn't know any of this until I was reading a criticism of the Royal Society of British Artists by Frank Rutter in one of the Sunday newspapers. He didn't like the show but finished off his review by saying something like, 'while there is nothing of special interest in this year's RBA there is in a window in Bond Street a painting which must be one of the great modern works of art.' It was all very exaggerated, very grand stuff, very flattering for a young man to read. Then I had a letter from Griggs. 'I knew you could etch', he said, 'but I didn't know you could paint. I've just seen a picture in Bond Street that I want to buy for the Tate and the Chantrey Trustees will meet next week so I will recommend that they see it before then.' Anyway, somewhere along the line something went wrong and someone went into the Fine Art Society and bought it (the painting) before the Trustees had their meeting. So Griggs wrote to me again and said that the Trustees had liked it and that I was to send another picture for them to see at the Royal Academy next year.*

Griggs was FLGriggs, the famous etcher and member of the Royal Academy who was one of the trustees of the Chantrey Bequest. This was a fund which had been endowed by Sir Francis Legatt Chantrey, who died in 1841. He was the son of a Sheffield carpenter and had worked as a grocer's boy before going on to become one of the country's leading sculptors. The bequest is used to purchase important works of sculpture and painting for the national galleries and any example of fine art so acquired is regarded as a national treasure. Such interest in one's work was, therefore, very flattering and underlined the ultimate success of the **Glencoe**

picture which, coming after the unsaleable **Assisi**, was to be a turning point in James's career. The painting has been described by one critic as probably one of the most important Scottish paintings of the 20th century. Today it hangs in the boardroom of Texas Instruments Incorporated in Dallas.

In the meantime the Chantrey Trustees, having had their appetite whetted by **Glencoe**, were anxious to consider the purchase of the next picture James submitted to the Royal Academy, but they weren't prepared to give him the luxury of the two years he had spent over the Highland epic. In fact they told him they wanted his next canvas by the closing date for submissions to the following exhibition in 1935, and that was only a few months away.

James set about his task immediately, the prospect of having a painting bought for the Tate being a powerful incentive to meet the deadline. He chose as his subject another snow scene, to be called **Winter in Angus** - indeed, winter with its subtle, subdued colours and tracery of defoliated trees was to be a favourite theme in his life's work. But this was also a mile-stone picture, the first big landscape he was to paint from his imagination - in contrast to **Assisi** and **Glencoe** which were actuality subjects - and it was to inspire what were to become known as the Four Seasons, captivating and meticulously executed portrayals of Scotland's domestic rural landscape at different times of the year, soon to be hailed as classics of their genre.

In **Winter in Angus** the foreground is dominated by Powrie Castle, built in the style of a French chateau on the northern edge of Dundee. But its relationship to the landscape, and the layout of that landscape, is pure fiction, an amalgam of other countryside features brought together in the studio to give an idealised composition.

**Glencoe** 1933-4   *Oil 31 x 41 Texas Instruments Incorporated, Dallas*

The artist himself explains: *The castle came because I had already made a painting and an etching of Powrie Castle and I thought it would make a good subject for a big picture. But in* **Winter in Angus** *I created an imaginary viewpoint up high. For the background - well I wanted a complicated background and at that time I was teaching on Fridays at Glenalmond and the background is the view from the Art Room window which I fitted in behind the castle. I was looking for something for the foreground and I decided to put in the pigeon loft but apart from that the rest of the foreground is just invented.* These synthesised pictures, formed out of random sketches, were to be his modus operandi for the next few years. They would be executed in a tight, crisp style verging on super-realism.

When **Winter in Angus** was duly acquired by the Chantrey Bequest one newspaper summed up Patrick's success this way:

> To have a picture purchased by the Chantrey Bequest is to win the Blue Riband of the Academy's year for any artist. It sets the seal on his work for all time. It places him among the immortals.

Immortal at 28! James, however, had no time to hang around on Cloud Nine and, at the suggestion of his agent Harold Dickens, followed up with the other three seasons in quick succession. Two of them, **Autumn, Kinnordy**, and **Midsummer in East Fife** - the latter bearing the stamp of a Constable - were territories close to Dundee, Kinnordy being the name of a private estate to the north of Kirriemuir in Angus and East Fife lying only across the Tay from the city. **Springtime in Eskdale**, however, was a less arbitrary choice of location. Eskdale is a district of Dumfriesshire in south west Scotland and was far flung from the artist's home patch.

It was Dickens himself who thought that Eskdale would be appropriate given that 1934 was the centenary of the death of Thomas Telford, the famous Scottish engineer who had been brought up in that airt, the son of a shepherd. The painting features the actual farmhouse where Telford was born in 1757 and from where he went out into the world to build bridges and roads and construct the great Caledonian

**Winter in Angus**  1935   *Oil 30 x 40 Tate Gallery, London*

**Autumn, Kinnordy** 1936   *Dundee Arts and Heritage, McManus Gallery/Bridgeman Art Library*

*30   Early Career*

**Midsummer in East Fife**  1936   *Oil 30 x 40 Aberdeen Art Gallery and Museums*

**Springtime in Eskdale**  1938  *Walker Art Gallery, Liverpool*

**An Exmoor Farm** *Ferens Art Gallery, Hull City Museums and Art Galleries UK/Bridgeman Art Library*

Canal. All the 'seasons' were hung at the Royal Academy and are now in major galleries, the route finally followed by **St Francis, Assisi** which was accepted for hanging after being almost entirely repainted, and then sold to the National Gallery of South Africa.

With his reputation now firmly established, paintings continued to flow from his easel, breath-taking panoramas often populated by people at work and at play. He was opening up the countryside in a most entrancing and instructive way to many town dwellers who were unable to fully explore the glories of nature for themselves in these days long before the mass ownership of cars. And despite his subject material being a mixture of various locations, many people were convinced they recognised, and had sometimes even worked on, a particular farm or were acquainted with a certain landscape, such was the easily identifiable way James captured the charisma of the rural scene on canvas.

All this illusion was perfectly harmless, of course, although on occasion it could lead to some confusion when the viewer discovered they had been "hoodwinked". This was the case with Sidney Gilliatt, a well-known film producer at that time who was looking for a farm to feature in one of his productions. Patrick's, **An Exmoor Farm**, shown at the Royal Academy in 1938, seemed to fit the bill. Gilliatt particularly wanted a farm location with a distant view of the sea and the Exmoor picture certainly included that with the Bristol Channel

OBAN Gateway to the Western Highlands and Islands

For official guide apply to Information Officer (Dept. M.C.) Municipal Buildings, Oban, Argyll

TRAIN SERVICES AND FARES FROM STATIONS, OFFICES AND AGENCIES · BRITISH RAILWAYS

featuring on the horizon. But when the producer visited the area he found there was no water to be seen. James had simply imported the sea as the means of composing a more interesting picture. Gilliatt must have been slightly miffed.

During this period James also painted a series of castles and country houses and from 1936 some of his commissions again took on a definite commercial flavour when his skills were hired by various mainline railway companies for posters and carriage panels. This diversion began when his painting of children sledging, **Sidlaw Village, Winter**, was purchased by the vice chairman of London Transport, who then asked James to design posters for the Underground and surface stations, offering idyllic views of town and country which could be reached by rail. Patrick's posters of Edinburgh from the castle, Loch Lomond, the Border abbeys and countryside, and the rivers Forth and Tay - together with his carriage panels of similar scenes displayed in the compartments before open-plan coaches were introduced much later – became familiar sights to millions of travellers.

Painting railway posters was a lucrative industry for many artists during the Thirties with generous retainers being paid by the companies. Today these early posters are valuable collector's pieces and fetch high prices at auction. At one time James's evocative poster of golfers at North Berwick for LNER (London and North Eastern Railway company) was valued at over £4000.

*James McIntosh Patrick marries Janet Watterston*

ALTHOUGH James Patrick was totally absorbed in his work, putting in long hours and becoming oblivious to the passage of time, he was not without interest in the opposite sex and had several girl friends before meeting and marrying the young woman who finally bowled him over. She was Janet Watterston, a slim and attractive secretary at University College, Dundee, then an adjunct of St Andrews University, where her father held the post of bursar. Coincidentally, her second cousin was the well-known landscape painter James Watterston Herald whose work adorned the walls in the office of Charles Soutar, the architect in partnership with James's father. These creations included watercolours and pastels which the young Patrick had often admired when visiting the premises. Now, in 1933, he was marrying into that side of the family.

Married life for the Patricks proceeded on an even keel throughout the remaining years of the Thirties. Andrew, the couple's first child, was born in 1934 and Ann, their daughter, completed the family three years later. James had no shortage of work, the Fine Art Society having said, following the **Glencoe** picture, that they would accept anything he cared to send them. So, financially he was now fairly well placed and at the beginning of 1939 felt able to transfer his family from their flat in the west end of the city to a fine Georgian manor house down by the river at Magdalen Green.

The house was called The Shrubbery and despite its elegance was not exactly the most sought after property in Dundee at that time. This had nothing to do with its location which was quite superb, the house being perched on the edge of a lovely stretch of common leading down to the banks of the Tay at a point where the Tay Bridge swings out from the landfall to stretch two miles across the river to the North shore of Fife. This is the bridge which carries the fame of its predecessor, caught up in calamity in December 1879, when it collapsed in a storm with the loss of 75 people who were pitched into the river when their train plunged through the fractured girders.

The new bridge takes exactly the same line as the old and is only a few hundred yards from the Shrubbery's front door, and it was precisely this proximity to the house that was so off-putting to prospective buyers. With a war very much in prospect many people felt that the bridge, a vital transport link down the east coast of Scotland, would be a prime target for enemy bombing with the Shrubbery likely to suffer collateral damage. But James and Janet took the plunge anyway and, in the event, the Luftwaffe paid scant attention to Dundee during the war that was to be declared in September of that year. Indeed, it was the the very location of the house that was to prove of great importance in the artist's future work, providing him with vistas, back and front, which were to be capitalised on canvas in a deeply significant way.

And yet this very nearly didn't happen. Three years earlier, in 1936, James had applied for the newly-created post of warden at Hospitalfield House, an extensive property on the outskirts of Arbroath, 15 miles from Dundee. This had originally been a 13th century leprosy and plague centre until eventually emerging from the mists of time as a Fine Art School for full-time students. Now it was about to change its role yet again, this time to become a post-graduate residential summer art school. The warden's job was really a sinecure, allowing the incumbent to continue with their private painting practice in return for acting as mentor to the students for a few months in the summer. The big 'perk' in this post was the rent-free accommodation in an idyllic setting, and this must have been a pleasing prospect for James who may by then have grown a little tired of life cooped up in a tenement flat with a young family. However, he failed to get the job, although for several years in the 1950's he was located at Hospitalfield during the summer

**Marion** 1935  *Oil 16 x 12 The Artist's Family*

months as visiting artist. But in 1939 James knew like everyone else that life was about to undergo great change.

LOOKING back over the first ten years of his career since graduating he had every reason to be satisfied. He had been able to earn his livelihood as a full-time artist in the most hostile of economic climates and, in the process, emerge as one of Scotland's most promising painters, exhibiting regularly at the Royal Scottish Academy and the Royal Academy in London. Apart from having been elected an Associate of the Royal Society of Painter-Etchers and Engravers, he had carried off the Guthrie Award in 1935, given each year by the RSA for the most meritorious picture by a young Scottish artist. His winning canvas had been a portrait entitled, **Marion**, a student at Dundee College of Art. He was now undoubtedly an artist in demand.

James's work, a good deal of it done in the West of Scotland, had also received much ecstatic publicity, with reviewers comparing his style and technique as a landscape painter with some of the great names of the past. They said that his paintings were influenced variously by Mantegna and other artists of the Italian 15th century; painters of the northern Renaissance such as Hugo van der Goes and, above all, Brueghel; the Old Masters generally, Constable, Turner and the Pre-Raphaelites. Reviewing his painting, **Ardmair Bay, Ross-shire**, one critic wrote somewhat portentously: *In its characteristics it suggests rather an*

**The Shrubbery** *painted by Robert Louden*

From his studio with the view which was a steady inspiration
*by kind permission of DC Thomson & Co Ltd, Dundee*

*influence from Japan than a slavish following of the French Impressionists.* He was bracketed with fellow Scots such as Fergusson, Cameron, Russell Flint, and Peploe. There is no doubt that James admired much of all this work and learned a good deal from it. Indeed, he readily admitted that the cattle and water in the foreground of **Midsummer in East Fife** had been influenced by Rubens in The Watering Place and that he had adopted Van Gogh's style of placing distinctive features, such as tufts of grass and other objects, close up at the front of landscapes to accentuate the realism of the painting.

But, as said already, James Patrick had never really been in any doubt about what he wanted to paint and how he wanted to paint it. Writing in the Artist magazine just before the war, Herbert Grimsditch said:

> His rise has been rapid. He seems to have known from the first what he wanted to do, and to have mastered with ease the technical knowledge necessary to its performance. He has been through no period of Sturm and Drang, no phase of fumbling, and he may be said to be as near 'a born artist' as it is possible to be.....There are moods in which one might prefer the swirling paint of a Dunlop, the shimmering light of a Lucien Pissarro, or that highly stylised decorative landscape that John Nash does so well. Yet for work like Patrick's there will always be a place, always a mood in which this seems the only way whereby to get the very essence of landscape.

Yes, James was going places. Then along came a man called Adolf Hitler to interrupt his progress.

# The War

JAMES PATRICK was 32 when the second world war broke out and, on account of his age and having never been a part-time soldier, sailor, or airman, he was not among the first to be called up for military service. It would be another nine months before he received his papers. In the meantime, although the British Expeditionary Force had gone to France to stem the German advance towards the Channel coast, activity on the home front was much less dramatic, giving rise to the term 'phoney' war.

Nevertheless, the signs of an emergency soon began appearing across the country with the evacuation of children, the mobilisation of the Home Guard (known initially as the Local Defence Volunteers and finally, and fondly, many years post-war, as 'Dad's Army'), the issue of ration books and gas masks, and the filling of sandbags. Women were being conscripted into the Land Army and drafted into munitions as well as the uniformed services. Military bases were sprouting up all over. Dundee was to have several seaplane bases in the Tay, naval anchorages in the harbour, and RAF stations across its hinterland. While James waited on his call to arms he tried to continue his painting as usual between spells as an air raid warden at a fortified post near his home.

But painting out of doors was no longer a free and easy occupation. The public was being bombarded with government posters warning that 'careless talk costs lives,' and to be on the lookout for enemy spies. Italians, who had long since settled in Scotland and were highly regarded in local communities, were whisked off to special camps for the duration when Benito Mussolini joined forces with Hitler. It was against this background of suspicion, then, that James was attempting to carry out his innocent work. But it was doomed to failure.

Each time he set up his easel away from the studio someone would 'phone the police, reporting that they had spotted a 'spy' drawing pictures for the other side. On several occasions a police car roared up on location to question him about his motives. During this period he was invited by the Pilgrim Trust to make a series of archival drawings of St.Andrews, but with aerial movements building up at RAF Leuchars nearby the project became increasingly embarrassing to carry through and James finally called a halt to outdoor work. For the foreseeable future, until he was in uniform, he would confine himself to barracks and concentrate on purely studio or other indoor subjects.

At that point he made an inspired choice of subject. It was so close to home it would have been understandable if he hadn't even thought about it. But one of James Patrick's great gifts was to spot a potential picture. He could tell instinctively at a glance if a particular scene would make an interesting painting, having become accustomed to viewing the world through an imaginary rectangle. Very seldom in a career that would span seventy years would he have to abort a picture because it wasn't going to work. And so, for his first real studio subject in his new house, he chose a setting which he gazed out upon from an upstairs window: his back garden. This might not have sounded like the most exciting material in the world but the result was to be a world class picture.

**A City Garden** shows Janet Patrick hanging washing out on a line with daughter Ann helping her mother to unload the clothes basket. Over the wall several factories and tenement blocks of houses, also with washings out to dry, reveal the closeness of city life. One can only imagine the thoughts going through the artist's mind as he painted this idyllic scene; the realisation that such domestic bliss as this was now under threat and might not survive the years ahead. These were precious days. The picture was hung at the Royal Academy in London, bought by Dundee Art Gallery, and later shown by invitation at exhibitions in Paris and Barcelona. It also provided an interesting talking point many years after the war when the Duke of Kent was lunching at Dundee City Chambers where the painting happened to be on display. After eyeing it closely his Royal Highness announced that a shirt on the line was hanging the wrong way, having been pinned up by the tail.

No-one present thought to challenge this opinion, in the belief perhaps that Dukes were experts at putting out a wash. But when Janet Patrick heard of the criticism she sounded off. *Please tell the gentleman,* she said firmly, *that shirts always dry more quickly if they are hung upside down.* She also gave the simple explanation for this. As the top part of the garment is the heaviest and, therefore, retains most moisture the shirt drips more quickly if suspended upside down and can be blown by the wind.

Following the success of the garden picture James turned his thoughts to his next project, a commission from Lady Lyell whose Kinnordy estate in Angus, at the back of Kirriemuir, was the location of the composite picture he had painted for his autumn theme in the Four Seasons. Lady Lyell now wanted him to paint a landscape incorporating Kinnordy Loch which lay close to the big house itself. This was really Lady Lyell's second choice of subject. She had originally wanted the artist to paint her husband, Charles Anthony Lyell, second Baron of Kinnordy, whom she had married in 1938 and was now a Lieutenant in the First Battalion, Scots Guards.

Like all wives whose husbands had gone off to war she feared for his safety and prayed for his safe return. In the meantime she wanted him to have his portrait painted by James Patrick whose earlier work she had admired so much. But the handsome young officer, then only 27, was in no mood for such self-indulgence, believing this to be a rather frivolous exercise at a time of war. James was, therefore, bent on painting the loch instead when he arrived at Kinnordy early in 1940. But no sooner had he unpacked his materials from the car when it started to snow, forcing him to shelter in the house where, much to his surprise, he came face to face with Lord Lyell. He was home on leave for a few days shooting but, like James, was being frustrated by the weather.

With both men under the same roof Lady Lyell realised she had the two components required for the portrait she so desired - the subject and the artist. Almost in the nature of a military manoeuvre, Lady

**A City Garden**  1940  *Oil 28 x 36 Dundee Arts and Heritage, McManus Gallery*

Lyell persuaded James to get busy with his sketch pad on her husband with as little fuss as possible while he waited impatiently in the drawing room for the skies to clear. Finding himself outflanked, His Lordship reluctantly agreed to pose on a shooting stick with a shot-gun tucked under his arm. The session went well but couldn't be repeated at Kinnordy on account of the officer having to rejoin his regiment at Chelsea Barracks. Shortly after, however, James travelled to London to complete the portrait at the Lyells' town house. He then returned to Kinnordy and painted the loch round the figure of Lord Lyell, making it appear that he was sitting within a few yards of the water. Much to the delight of the family, James had managed to merge both subjects on the one canvas. Lady Lyell had won hands down!

The artist was never to see Lord Lyell again. Three years later in North Africa James was on a troop train travelling from Algiers to Tunis when he spotted several Scots Guards officers who had been wounded and were returning to their units from the base hospital. *Any word of Lord Lyell?*, he asked anxiously, knowing that the Guards had been in the front line. *I'm afraid so*, replied one of the officers. *He was killed in action last week.* James was stunned as the train continued to rattle through the shimmering heat of the desert.

Meanwhile, back in Scotland, there had been a fierce April storm in Angus which had brought down the telephone lines at Kinnordy House, as a result of which all urgent business connected with the estate was being conducted by telegram. On this particular day there was a batch of the buff-coloured envelopes delivered to the big house in mid-morning. Lady Lyell began going through the pile, opening each envelope without paying a great deal of attention to the way they were addressed. She was working her way through the messages in this fashion when suddenly she froze. The text of the telegram in her hand hit her like a thunderbolt. It was from the War Office and it began with the dreaded words: 'We deeply regret to inform you....,' and went on to explain that Lord Lyell had been killed in action in North Africa.

Later Lady Lyell was told how her husband had lost his life while displaying outstanding gallantry during an engagement lasting several days, culminating in his death when he successfully led a charge on a German gun position at Dejebel Boul Aoukas. For this he was posthumously awarded the Victoria Cross. His son, the present Lord Lyell, was only four when he lost his father. Lady Lyell has been a widow ever since. The portrait of her husband by James Patrick takes pride of place in her sitting room.

**Captain The Lord Lyell VC**  1940  *Oil 36 x 28 The Lady Lyell*

IT WAS May, 1940, just before the British Expeditionary Force began its miracle evacuation from Dunkirk, that Mr James McIntosh Patrick was enlisted into the army to become almost overnight, Private James McIntosh Patrick, with a number he would never forget. His call-up papers arrived at The Shrubbery on a lovely early summer's morning as he was working in his studio, putting the finishing touches to a landscape showing the sleepy village of Glamis nestling in the valley of Strathmore. Andrew and Ann gathered round their mother's skirts as their father announced with a heavy heart that he would be leaving them within a few days. It was a scene being repeated all over Britain at the time but his departure was none the easier for that. He was under orders to report to Catterick, the huge training camp in north Yorkshire where he would be assigned to the 5lst Training Regiment, Royal Armoured Corps.

No-one can recall whether he had given his occupation as self-employed artist or self-employed painter. If it was the latter he could have finished up giving the latrines a fresh coat of paint. In the event his "cover" was blown when copies of railway posters he had completed months before were sent on to him at Catterick by the various companies who had commissioned the work. Soon these posters were decorating the mess halls and it wasn't long before word got round about Private Patrick's artistic ability. In no time at all he was told to report to the chief instructor.

The army authorities had been concerned for some time about the lack of entertainment in the Catterick area, particularly on the camp itself, and had now decided to make good this deficit by converting an empty hut into a make-shift theatre. There was no lack of volunteers among those who had been tradesmen in civvy street and James didn't complain either when told he would be in charge of painting the sets. The accommodation, however, was rather cramped and Private Patrick had to devise a system of having several sets on stage throughout each show, but only bringing them into use when required. He managed this by painting various scenes on a series of revolving curtains, a system which he later declared was revolutionary. Whether or not he had broken new ground in scenery production was never confirmed. There was, however, no doubting the innovative nature of his mind, a capacity for making do with limited materials to achieve maximum effect. This would serve him well in all sorts of minor ways throughout his life as an artist. But the theatre, which specialised in reviews with cast members also drawn from the ranks, became a great success and proved yet again the remarkable array of talent available within a conscripted army.

Between these thespian activities James had been training as a tank driver, but after several months at Catterick the army put two and two together and informed him they were to harness his skills as a landscape painter in a more worthwhile fashion by commissioning him into the Camouflage Corps. It was early the following year, 1941, before his commission came through. He remembered the day well. That morning he had decided to celebrate his promotion by lying a bit longer in bed. This, however, was like a red rag to a bull when the squad sergeant came striding into the barracks, yelling at the top of his voice and ordering James to appear on the defaulters' parade. The artist loved telling the story of how strange it had been getting up eventually that morning as an acting lance-corporal and walking out the camp gates several hours later as a lieutenant. Later

**Lieutenant James McIntosh Patrick**

he was to reflect thus on his new function in the military machine:

*There were a lot of direct commissions of artists into the Camouflage Corps, several of whom were well known then or have since become quite famous. We all knew how artists like Wadsworth had been involved with painting the Dazzle ships during the First World War but what I had to do was totally different. My CO had written the classic text book on animal camouflage which showed how animals not only adapted their colours to harmonise with their background but also modified their behaviour so as not to draw attention to themselves, and that's basically what military camouflage is about.*

*I remember when I had just left Training School how we had to prepare for any retaliation for the Dieppe Raid which was being planned. We had to build bases for mobile anti-aircraft guns and it was my job to camouflage these bases, huge plugs of concrete in the fields. First I had to persuade the gunners to position their guns at the edges of the fields where there was natural cover from hedges and trees. Then I had to make sure that the contractors, with their huge lorries, used the fields in the same way a farmer would. A farmer doesn't cross the middle of his fields, he sticks to the side, so I had to make the drivers think like farmers. All their tracks, when seen from the air, looked like farm vehicle tracks, driving around the edge of the fields. That's a simple example but it shows how I was able to use my knowledge of what happened on a farm.*

When Lieutenant Patrick arrived in North Africa in 1942, however, the desert conditions obviously called for a different set of camouflage techniques. There was no way you could hide a tank in the desert no matter what colour or pattern you might apply to it, but you could mislead the enemy into believing you had a much smaller number than you were really deploying. This was done with nets and other materials which would eliminate shadows and convey false impressions on aerial photographs. James himself devised a colour pattern for the gun barrels of the Allied tanks which made them appear much shorter to the enemy, thereby disguising their true fire power until brought into action. This subterfuge out-foxed the forces of Field Marshall Rommel and earned Lieutenant Patrick a mention in despatches.

When the North African campaign ended in victory in May, 1943, James was attached to 1st Army Headquarters in the romantic ruins of ancient Carthage, the former capital of Roman Africa. By now the First Army was disbanding in preparation for the next offensive and James, not belonging to any particular unit, found himself without duties of any kind. His tent was pitched near the palace of the Bey of Tunis, hard by the Mediterranean Sea and not far from the picturesque Arab town of Sidi Bou Sa'i'd. The scenery in this area was ready made for an artist, the gleaming white houses with blue and green shutters contrasting with the harsh red rock. Having virtually not painted for almost three years, James armed himself with materials bought in Tunis and set to work with a vengeance.

During the next six weeks he painted non-stop, putting together a portfolio of some of the best watercolours he was to produce: pictures of historic ruins, street scenes, the sea and distant Cap Bon, and the exteriors and interiors of the houses occupied by a resident colony of French artists with whom he became very friendly. Finally, when the army required his services again, he was posted back to Algiers to join the camouflage staff at General Eisenhower's headquarters. He was there for several months working on concealment and deception planning for the Sicily landings and the greater Italian campaign that was to follow.

Although the fighting had come to an end in North Africa, there was still plenty of drama to be had in that former theatre of war. One day James was working in his office when suddenly there was a huge explosion at the nearby docks. A consignment of German anti-tank mines – supposedly deactivated – were being loaded on a ship taking them back to Britain for training purposes when a cargo net snapped as one batch was being winched aboard. As the mines crashed on to the dockside they went off with a mighty roar, creating a chain of further detonations as the other mines stacked nearby also exploded. This incident destroyed a large part of the docks. A week later the harbour was hit by another devastating accident when a ship carrying phosphorus caught fire. Again James was an eye witness as a cloud of white smoke mushroomed into the sky. As a destroyer, along with several tugs and fire tenders, attempted to move the stricken vessel away from the harbour there was a violent explosion which rocked the coastline for miles. When the smoke finally cleared there wasn't a ship to be seen. They had all been sunk without trace. Both these tragedies cost thousands of lives.

*Sketching the sea North Africa    Love from Pat*

**The Amphitheatre, Santa Maria, Capua**
*By kind permission of Eduardo Alessandro Studios, Broughty Ferry*

Several months later James was assigned to the School of Military Engineering which was being established at Bone, just along the coast from Algiers, where he was put in command of the camouflage wing with a staff of several other artists. For the first time in his army life he was part of a team rather than a lone staff officer being sent to different locations as the need for his expertise arose. By the end of 1943, with the Italian campaign now well under way in the face of an Allied advance, the school was transferred to Capua, 25 miles north of Naples. Here James set about devising courses to meet the camouflage demands of a European environment which, of course, were much different from those of a desert campaign, and sometimes his needs caused friction in the camp. Remarking on this years after he said: *It's silly, but one of the biggest problems I ever had was when I was in charge of the Camouflage Division at Capua. I used to drill the troops as to how they should black-up and decorate their helmets with twigs and dull down all the shiny bits on their webbing and rifles. Then they had to turn up for guard duty with blancoed belts and gaiters because their CSM refused to let his men go on duty 'unless they were a credit to the regiment'. I was trying to stop them getting killed and he was more concerned with regimental pride and honour. It's a funny thing, the army mind.*

But compared to North Africa, Capua was a much more congenial posting. High Command had decreed that every effort should be made to provide base camp with an ambience as different to battle conditions as possible. This allowed James to develop his talents for interior decoration with the mess halls, common rooms, and bars all being done up in attractive colours and different motifs. He still found time, however, to slip away occasionally into the surrounding country for painting expeditions of his own. By now he had met up with the famous painter and teacher, Captain William Coldstream, later to be knighted and become Slade Professor of Fine Art at University College, London. Unlike Patrick, Coldstream was not involved in the disguising of military hardware. He was an official war artist, but still welcomed the opportunity of painting other subjects along with James, who now held the rank of major. When it came to acquiring his painting materials, the Dundee artist was surprised to find he could purchase British paints in local shops, these being particularly popular with Italian artists. Even more intriguingly, these were the same paints that were being bought by German soldiers only weeks earlier, before they were forced to retreat.

THROUGHOUT the war James and Janet Patrick, in common with other couples, exchanged hundreds of letters, correspondence which played a vital part in sustaining morale during long periods, sometimes years, of separation. In one of his letters home James was able to describe a spectacular incident in 1944 which had nothing to do with the war and was, therefore, given scant publicity. This was a major eruption at Mount Vesuvius which was only 20 miles from Capua. Flames could be seen leaping from the crater with great columns of smoke towering over it during the day. Huge deposits of volcanic dust and ash buried entire villages in the lee of the mountain, with Pompeii also suffering much damage. Fortunately much of the dust was blown out to sea and actually ended up in North Africa. James had seen all this at first hand and was never to forget the devastation of it all.

Many of his letters home reflected on the life he had left behind and it was obvious that his thoughts were never far from his family and the gentle, rolling contours of the Scottish countryside. From North Africa he had once written: *As I gaze across the arid desert in the mid-day heat I think of the cool summer breezes moving through the Carse of Gowrie with all its farms and bonny country roads lined with trees. Hasten the day when I can once more be with my loved ones and set up my easel below more familiar skies.*

James was stationed in Capua until after the end of the war at which point the engineering school became a technical college where tradesmen due for release could be put through refresher courses. To make this work as realistic as possible, houses and shops were built and a whole street constructed. Men had their hair cut in a salon which would have held its own in Mayfair. On the wall of one bathroom James painted a big mural of huge angel fish which sparkled like gold. Within a matter of days the place became known as "Cleopatrick's Bath". It was the most bizarre painting he ever did.

The war had also resulted in another curious artistic legacy inherited by many of his comrades in arms. From his time at Catterick onwards he had drawn, by popular demand, sketches of the men he had served with. Starting with his squad sergeant, he progressed through the ranks, right up to brigadiers and generals. These pencil and ink portraits were sent back to loved

ones at home and were treasured by families long after the war had finished. But how many of the grandchildren who have inherited this artwork realise the identity of the artist? *I did the drawings free of charge and in return was given various favours*, James recalled when his army days were behind him.

Overall, James could be said to have had a "good war", an oxymoron which simply meant that he had survived in one piece, had adapted well to military life, and had to a large extent profited from the experience in a way which would stand him in good stead in civilian life. In his case the painting he had been able to undertake in uniform was to change the whole course of his career back in Dundee.

In North Africa and Italy he had been forced to abandon his previous technique of composing landscapes in the studio from a variety of sketches, creating a 'synthetic' picture which was largely the product of his own imagination and didn't constitute any one particular scene. But during the war he had no studio, and in any case could not have afforded the time necessary for preliminary sketches. Everything had to be done out of doors, often within earshot of gunfire and, with speed being of the essence, James discovered he was more or less able to complete a painting during a single session. This was also made possible by his use of watercolour instead of oil, the former being a much quicker medium in which to work and requiring less kit bag space for the materials.

All these factors combined to open James Patrick's eyes to a totally new approach to method and style, that of a 'plein air' painter.

# Career Resumed

**B**EFORE the Second World War, and for many years after it, there was a famous columnist who wrote in the Daily Mirror under the name of Cassandra. He was William - later Sir William - Connor and he was the scourge of the Establishment. When he returned to his desk in Fleet Street after demob in 1946 he restarted his column with the immortal opening line: *As I was saying when I was interrupted....,* creating the impression that his absence had been no more than a nuisance, but now he was back and it was business as usual.

This was much the same attitude that ex-Major James Patrick also assumed when he, too, picked up the threads of his previous career, roughly at the same time as Cassandra was winning back his readers. The artist was anxious to re-establish himself as quickly as possible, and what better way to do that than with an exhibition. It had been previously arranged with his agent Harold Dickens that his wartime paintings in North Africa and Italy, with a smattering of work done previously in Scotland, would be shown, first in London and then in Dundee, Edinburgh, and Glasgow. The opening exhibition in the capital, held in the New Bond Street Gallery of the Fine Art Society, was heralded by a banner across the front of the building with the artist's name "up in lights." After

six years of anonymity Patrick could be forgiven a glow of pleasure at finding himself back on a public platform. The event itself was a resounding success with a high percentage of sales and was given the royal stamp of approval with a personal visit by Queen Mary, the Queen Mother. The follow-up exhibitions also resulted in a great flourish of cheque books, to such an extent that the Glasgow venue had to be cancelled through lack of paintings.

These exhibitions were, in a sense, a watershed in the career of the artist by demonstrating the popularity of his new approach to painting, albeit one that had been forced upon him by wartime conditions - although the pictures themselves were not war subjects, but depicted scenes which gave little indication of the conflict that had taken place. A further exhibition of his watercolours by the Fine Art Society in 1948 confirmed the success of his new style and in that year he painted the last of his composite pictures, **An Angus Farm**, which was shown at the Royal Academy.

He had by now crossed the Rubicon, forming a more intimate relationship with the countryside and Mother Nature, reinforcing his belief in a force stronger than his own. James Patrick - who had for some considerable time been styling himself J.McIntosh Patrick to avoid confusion with another artist of the same name – was now leaving home every morning to paint outside on location, taking the countryside as he found it without the need to artificially rearrange things as before; subjects which, much to his surprise, existed in such profusion within the hinterland of Dundee that he would only rarely stray outwith a 15-mile radius of the city for the rest of his days.

His work would bear testimony to place names in Perthshire and Angus, and sometimes Fife, meriting only small print on big maps but which he would immortalise in the titles of his paintings: **Knapp, Dron, Tullybaccart, Carse of Gowrie, Longforgan, Kingoodie, Birkhill, Rossie Priory, Kinnaird, Auchterhouse, Abernyte, Glamis, Airlie, Balruddery, Murroes, Lundie, Kinfauns, Kirkmichael, Balmerino,** and countless other picturesque spots which would gradually become familiar to his army of admirers in many lands. McIntosh Patrick would continue to paint occasionally in the Highlands, particularly when on rare family holidays, but Nature in the raw didn't hold the same excitement for him and soon began to pall beneath his brush. He was always glad to return to the east coast where man had wrought his hand in domesticating the countryside with farm buildings and drystane dykes; corn stooks, fences, and tree-lined roads; small bridges, cultivated fields, and neat hedge rows. These features would become the hallmark of his future work, the Angus and Perthshire hills providing the perfect backdrop to the rolling farmlands neatly set out in distinctive Scottish style.

The man himself put it this way some time later: *As I got to know the countryside better and better, I came to realise that rhythmic ideas are inside you and so you go around looking for landscapes where the countryside fits a pre-conceived idea that you have inside you and which you recognise when you see it. In other words, a twisted bit of wood, a wall or a gate, immediately causes you to say, 'Ah, that's the bit I'm looking for'.*

*Now if you go back and look at my early pictures, which were made up in the studio, you'll find that they are the same only I didn't realise at that time that you could find what you wanted in Nature. It DOES exist and you CAN find the same arrangements in the countryside and I don't have to invent them anymore. Realism, or naturalism, is much more difficult than what I was painting in the 1930's. It's much easier in lots of ways to make up a picture than to paint Nature as it appears before us. Despite this, I still do it because I grew towards it and now can't stop. I think I'm just a realist, that's all....of a certain kind of subject. I don't suppose there's much sentimentality about my paintings but I have a deep feeling that Nature is immensely dignified when you're out of doors. I'm struck by the dignity of everything.*

This transformation in his work was not without its practical problems. He had to master the technique of completing a picture within the same set of climatic conditions, a difficult feat given the capricious nature of the Scottish weather and one calling for a swift painting hand. This was to say nothing of the discomfort he had to suffer in a studio open to the skies; having to cope with snow, sleet and frost, wind, rain and the changing patterns of light and shade. His hands became those of a bricklayer, chapped and gnarled, and the hazards of a dripping nose close to an easel are obvious to any artist.

Dressing for the outdoors in the winter, especially for an occupation engaging in so little body movement - and working with materials which freeze in low temperatures - posed several challenges, but of a type which the artist's sense of improvisation was

**Burnside**  *Dundee Arts and Heritage, McManus Gallery*

able to largely overcome. Glycerine in the mixing water acted as an anti-freeze while a primus stove below the easel, anchored with a brick at the end of a rope to withstand the wind, kept the palette from congealing. His wind-breaks made Heath Robinson's contraptions look like models of orthodoxy. One pole would be attached to a fence or a tree, the other to a bumper on his car, with the sheet lashed to wheel hubs or a wing mirror. If all else failed he would simply throw up the tailgate and work below its shelter. Only monsoon conditions would drive him indoors.

As for his own comfort he once said when asked how he kept warm: *I don't, I just keep cold*. This wasn't quite true, although wearing only mitts to keep his hands reasonably free meant his fingers would often be so cold they were unable to unscrew the caps of his paint tubes. He did, however, have the rest of his body well happed up in double layers of clothing with scarves, fur boots, thick woollen socks, and a fur hat with ear flaps. If the wind was noisy he plugged his ears with cotton wool. He once tried painting a winter scene from a window inside a nearby building but soon gave up. Only when he went outside into two feet of snow and a frost-laden wind did he find the stimulation to make the picture start to work. There was now no substitute for communing with nature, although looking at any of his wintry landscapes one never gets the impression that the artist suffered physical discomfort during the painting process. By and large he found outdoor work to be healthy. *The weather hasn't killed me yet*, he would say cheerfully.

But dressing the way he did to keep out the cold often gave him the appearance of being a tramp, and there were several occasions when a farmer would

**A Winter Day**

come striding across a field and order him off his land - only then to finish up buying the picture when realising who the visitor was. One such farmer studied the painting of his farm with amazement. *Ye, ken,* he finally said, pushing back his bonnet, *eh've been here for forty years and eh never realised the place looked sae bonny.* And with that he whipped the uncompleted picture off the easel, saying he liked it just the way it was before marching off to get his money.

There were other hazards, too, that had to be faced out of doors, with pictures being blown off the easel or being scratched on bushes while being carried to and from his car. One of the more serious accidents happened when he was working on the final stages of a large watercolour which wouldn't dry quickly enough in the humidity of a hot summer's day. To overcome this he held the drawing board face down over a paraffin heater. But when the painting worked loose it caught fire and one of his favourite pieces of work was totally destroyed. His other drying method, which caused much consternation to onlookers, was to ignite a rolled-up newspaper and swish the flames back and forwards across the canvas. Timidity was not part of his make-up.

Then there was the day he was painting at Kinfauns, just outside Perth, when he heard the sound of gunfire. Suddenly a couple of shots thudded into the tree he was working under, covering him in a shower of broken twigs. Having survived the war he didn't relish being wiped out on the lower slopes of a Scottish hill. At that moment a gamekeeper came crashing through the bushes full of apologies. He had been shooting at some pigeons.

THE COURIER AND ADVERTISER, SATURDAY, FEBRUARY 15, 1930.

A DUNDEE CLOSE    Specially Drawn by J. M'Intosh Patrick.

**In the garden with Sam**

whenever they came across an attractive rural aspect. This, of course, was innocent nonsense and the artist would chuckle at the thought of being considered superior to the Great Creator. *This is all very flattering,* he once said, *but I suppose if you went to some parts of Sussex it would remind you of Constable, or if you went to Provence it would remind you of Van Gogh. I just know that I'm happy painting in the sun. Sometimes that hymn comes to me and I turn round to Sam and say: 'Well, Sam, the world is very beautiful and full of joy today'.* Sam was his Labrador.

This illusion of supernatural power can be partly explained when you look at a McIntosh Patrick landscape. The artist creates a remarkable 3D effect which draws you right into the picture. Suddenly you find yourself standing in that actual setting and feel you are about to set out on a country ramble without ever setting foot outside. He achieves this sense of transfer through meticulous attention to scale and perspective, making certain that every feature is in proper proportion to everything else. Often he would draw a grid on a preparatory sketch to make certain the positioning of everything was exactly right. He was attracted to the element of space in his paintings and one day, standing on a ridge near Abernyte overlooking the Carse of Gowrie, he described this concept with great enthusiasm: *These trees just in front of us are only a few yards away; the next lot are a hundred yards further on; then there are fields for 15 miles or so and beyond that a range of hills. We can see all this by just standing here. But in my pictures I attempt to give you exactly the same feeling of depth. You walk down a road, open a gate, cross a field, climb over a dyke and so on.*

The viewer is invariably drawn into the painting in the first place by the simple expedient of a road or lane, a stream or a line of trees, winding into the

B Y THE early 1950's the new style of his land-scapes was becoming instantly recognisable to an increasing section of the public. With their accuracy of vision and wonderful draughtsmanship, these paintings captured the countryside with such realism that many people, in a state of euphoric admiration, were now paying him the ultimate compliment of believing it was he who had created the wonders of Nature by referring to 'a McIntosh Patrick scene' landscape from the foot of the picture. All you do is to take one step forward and you're there. The artist has provided you with a natural point of entry.

This sense of 'being there' is described by Gordon Dilworth, of Pitlochry, who recalls visiting an art exhibition mounted by the Clydesdale Bank at their Glasgow headquarters during the city's European Year of Culture and being inspired by a Patrick landscape. *The day had been dull, the background was a nondescript wood and the subject in the foreground was newly ploughed land, standing wet. It was emphatically a painting, not a photograph, as you could feel the sodden furrows under your wellies and smell the damp earth. The marble hall in St. Vincent Place had vanished under McIntosh Patrick's spell. Dr Patrick may not have asked his viewers hard intellectual questions but, even at first glance, his pictures excite the imagination and raise the spirits through their compostion and his skill with shapes, colours and textures.*

Trees were certainly the great love of his life as an artist, and many critics agree that no-one could express their majesty and delicate tracery as he could. He would spend hours recreating them in almost all his paintings, according them the status of portraits. He considered trees to be one of nature's great gifts, marvelling at the height they grew in defiance of gravity and then being able to hold aloft a mass of branch and leaf of such considerable weight. He would never attempt to draw or paint a tree from memory, requiring always to look at one as he captured the rhythm of its infrastructure. He was always appalled at the way trees were so often needlessly chopped down, thereby spoiling the character of a beauty spot, and he always hoped that by expressing them so vividly in his paintings people would treat them with greater respect. *Trees are like human beings in a way*, he would always say. *I consider trees to be friends.* He constantly persuaded farmers to plant more trees, if only because they prevented gale-force winds from flattening crops and helped to raise the temperature in the fields they sheltered.

As an artist his powers of observation were acute to a degree which eluded most other people. And yet he always maintained that others, too, could enjoy a deeper appreciation of their environment. *The success of these pictures of mine*, he said, *arises from the fact they are about life. A tremendous amount of modern painting is about art whereas the pictures I am painting are about the world around us. If you are on this earth and you get pleasure from the actual environment, from the actual world; if you don't wish the trees were red and the grass was pink and so on; if you like it the way it is then this comes a lot from understanding something of what goes on in Nature. Don't just refer to the roses and the sky. Really look at the roses and really look at the sky and you will get great pleasure from doing this.*

With his new approach to painting quickening up the whole process, McIntosh Patrick was able to step up his output considerably from its pre-war level of between six to ten paintings a year. Now he could sometimes produce 36 pictures a year. Very often he would be working on two canvasses simultaneously, making sure that if weather conditions weren't giving him the effects he required for one he could switch to the other and thus use his time most profitably. He was able to work this system throughout his life, painting until he was almost 90, on account of two attributes: his robust health - he was as tough as old boots - and a deeply ingrained work ethic. He never shirked a day's work and would never hang around waiting for inspiration. In that sense painting was like any other occupation. He simply got on with it every day, irrespective of bio-rhythms, weather, domestic problems, or minor ailments. Having completed one picture he would immediately get the car out and cruise around until quickly identifying another landscape subject.

On these occasions, when accompanied by a passenger, he would provide continuous commentary on the nobility of the countryside, thereby putting his driving into the hair-raising category.

There was, however, one famous painting whose location required no clocking up of mileage. As with his outstanding garden picture painted from a rear window in his house, the artist now took further advantage of another scene which could be viewed from The Shrubbery. There it was, stretching out below him across Magdalen Green to the Fife hills beyond, a panorama which was to become his most popular painting of all in reproduction form, **Tay Bridge from my Studio Window.** In 1940, **A City Garden**, was an expression of hope that the happiness of home life would survive the uncertainties of war. But now he was safely back with his family and what better way to celebrate that reunion than to paint Dundee's most famous structure in its glorious river setting, a symbol of home for all returning Dundonians, the very bridge he himself had crossed only a short time before when finally leaving his army days behind.

The painting possibly embraced more activity than any other he did, although many of his landscapes would be populated to a lesser extent. But on this canvas two trains can be seen on the bridge with much shunting going on at the sidings on the Dundee landfall, while a cargo vessel sails up the river. In the road outside the house there is also plenty of interest. Janet, his wife, is at the front gate having returned from some shopping with Lulu their dog; Andrew is on his bicycle; David McDonald, a Dundee stockbroker, is walking a pack of dogs; Roy, a local fruit merchant, is passing with his horse-drawn van; there is a pedestrian, a figure on a bench and a woman out walking with a pram. The identity of the mother and child is unknown to this day. She was simply passing at the time. But many wives were convinced it was they who were in the picture - claims which were backed up by many fathers too.

Even the name of the fruiterer, although known to the artist, caused much speculation long after the painting was exhibited at the Royal Academy in 1948. One morning many years later McIntosh Patrick was having breakfast when the 'phone rang. It was a Dundee man who had emigrated to Tasmania and was at that very moment entertaining visitors in his home where the Tay Bridge picture was featured on his living room wall. They were arguing over the identity of the van owner. Could Mr Patrick supply the answer? When he told him it was Mr Roy there was a loud groan down the line from the other side of the world. *Damn it, I've lost my bet*, shouted the man. *I was sure it was someone else.* And with that he banged down the phone in Tasmania. Another point of debate centred round the railings and gates of the house. These had been removed for the munitions effort at the start of the war and, although never replaced, were painted in by Patrick to enhance the overall composition by casting an interesting shadow pattern across the garden path. They also reminded him of the property's original state, but the inclusion of the ironwork inevitably confused sightseers who later came to browse at the location. The artist would paint other scenes from his house, back and front, but none would have quite the same impact as the Tay Bridge in 1948.

**Tay Bridge from my Studio Window**  1948  *Oil 30 x 40 Dundee Arts and Heritage, McManus Gallery*

AS McIntosh Patrick's popularity soared through-out the 50's and 60's - indeed, it was never to go into decline - his universal appeal struck a somewhat sour note with many of those who occupied the loftier regions of the art establishment. They believed he was cashing in on public demand for pretty pictures - "chocolate box art" was the pejorative term often used - and by doing so was guilty of "watering down" his previous, more academic, style which had won him such acclaim through the **Four Seasons**, **Glencoe**, and other pictures of that genre. He was also accused of producing 'photographic' art. The artist handled such criticism with calm assurance: *I don't worry about that. I've never taken a photograph in my life. I've never owned a camera. My paintings are realism and realism was there before cameras. My pictures are honest, not arty. I paint the world as it is.....people say I'm copying nature. Well, I wish I could. Wouldn't it be wonderful to be the equal of nature?. Nobody can do that. People who think that about my work have never looked at nature. No, it's just plain silly.*

This so-called abandonment of high-brow art for something less intellectual was best commented upon at the time by Charles Carter in a magazine article he wrote in 1951 while Director of Aberdeen Art Gallery:

> There may be some who will look askance at such popularity; we are so accustomed to regarding the popular artist as a pot-boiler. Because many artistically worthless paintings have been popular we make the mistake of assuming that all popular paintings must be bad. The unrecognised of one generation have so often become the darlings of the next, whilst giants of the exhibition galleries have been as pygmies when transferred to the hall of fame, that we are reluctant to use the ready sale of an artist's work and his election to the academies as yardsticks by which to measure his achievement.
>
> And we are right. Artistic merit is not to be judged by such things. Disregarding them, it is always posterity which will award the laurels, laying them upon the tomb and not the brow of the artist; but his contemporaries cannot neglect such tangible evidence nor, because they must live, can artists. I recall hearing of two artists who were discussing the merits of their respective works in an exhibition. After one had referred to the abstract qualities and superior artistic merits of his own work, the other finally clinched the matter by saying: 'Yes, but I've sold mine'. It has not yet become an inevitable condemnation of a painting that it has found a buyer.

Patrick's work certainly sold. With the art market enjoying an unprecedented boom on a popular front with the creation of jobs and growth of house ownership, the Dundee artist was unable to keep pace with commissions. He had a book full of names which he constantly consulted with a worried frown, once remarking that even if he was to keep on painting until he could paint no more he would still be unable to fulfil all his commitments. This turned out to be a self-fulfilling prophecy. The trouble was he kept selling his pictures to admirers who would spot them taking shape on the easel and coax him into a premature sale. His son Andrew, who joined the Fine Art Society in 1954 and became managing director in 1972, explains that although his firm had long since been his father's agent they saw very little of his work. He put it thus in a radio programme in February, 1982: *He's far more pleased to let someone have a picture if they really want it than to actually find the best possible market for it. If someone arrives at the house and says they would like a painting for a wedding present or something he'll let them have it. He is choosing someone who actually wants something rather than a position he can't control.*

Many people have built up collections of Patrick's work over the years, never tiring of his landscapes or regretting their investment. Two such aficionados have their own McIntosh Patrick galleries six thousand miles apart in vividly contrasting settings: Sandy Saddler, who lives in the Scottish country town of Forfar set in the type of Angus landscape favoured by the artist, and Dr Ken Borchardt, whose home in California is a leisurely Cadillac run from the Golden Gate Bridge of San Francisco.

Sandy was one of the world's finest amateur golfers during the 1960's, captaining the Scottish team for many years and playing three times against America in the British Walker Cup side. He was the Walker Cup skipper for the 1977 meeting at Long Island and the year before had led Britain to victory in bringing home the Eisenhower Trophy. The golfing maestro had first admired a McIntosh Patrick painting in a friend's house in the late 1970's, bought one at auction shortly after, and has been hooked on his work ever since. On one occasion he took a Patrick oil to the artist's house to show him his latest acquisition. The painting was badly in need of a clean and much to Sandy's consternation his host put it under a running tap in the bathroom and began scrubbing the canvas down with a nail brush. *You'll ruin it!* cried the golfer, suffering the sort of agony he associated with missing a nine-inch putt. *The oil is as hard as rock,* Patrick assured him, going on to restore the picture's original sparkle.

Sandy runs the family bakery business in Forfar where the adjoining tearoom - called the Gallery Tearooms - accommodates the overspill of his Patrick collection on the walls above the tables. The menus carry reproductions of the artist's work and you can order up a McIntosh Patrick pizza from the kitchen. *From the time we met my golf started going downhill,* jokes Sandy. *I found him to be a fascinating man and spent much time in his company instead of being out on the course!*

Meanwhile, in Novato, California, Ken Borchardt mulls over his McIntosh Patricks almost every day. He also made initial contact with the artist in 1977. During the first trip he and his wife, Joyce, paid to Scotland that year he spotted one of his landscapes in an Edinburgh exhibition and was so captivated by the painting that he drove to Dundee to meet the artist himself, subsequently forming a friendship which has brought him and his wife back to Scotland many times. *His paintings and fellowship have given us great joy and although we often tried to coax him into visiting us in San Francisco he would never leave his beloved Scotland,* says Ken, now the research director of a bio-chemical company. The Borchardts are the owners of the only picture painted jointly by McIntosh Patrick and his daughter, Ann, also a well-known professional artist. It is a still life, **Mums and Fruit**, in which the father painted the flowers and the daughter dealt with the fruit.

**Sandy Saddler**
*Left:* In his golfing heyday
*Below left:* With customers in his Gallery Tearoom
*Below:* Where the menu pays tribute to many Scots artists

Our Pizzas are thin based, approx. 10 inches
and are freshly baked to order on the premises.

**McINTOSH PATRICK**
Fresh Tomatoes / Mozzarella Cheese – £2.50

**McTAGGART**
Ham / Pineapple / Mozzarella Cheese – £3.00

**McCLURE**
Onion / Mozzarella Cheese – £2.50

**MOROCCO**
Mushrooms / Mozzarella Cheese – £2.50

**HERRALD**
Tuna / Mozzarella Cheese – £3.00

**MORRISON**
Pepperoni or Salami / Peppers / Mozzarella Cheese – £3.50

**LAMOND**
Chilli con Carne / Mozzarella Cheese – £3.50

**CADENHEAD**
Bolognaise / Mozzarella Cheese – £3.50

Side Salad – £1.00

Portion of Coleslaw – 80p

Extra Toppings can be ordered at 80p each

All prices include VAT

**Mums and Fruit**  *see page 61*

**Mr & Mrs Ken Borchardt**
*at home in California*
*with some of their collection*

**Glamis Castle 1960** *HRH The Princess Margaret*

His paintings, in fact, are to be found everywhere. For many years an important work was bought by a leading public gallery from the walls of the Royal Academy and other prestigious exhibitions. Royal palaces also have their share of McIntosh Patricks. Princess Margaret was given a painting of Glamis Castle, her birthplace, as a wedding present in 1960 from the people of Angus, and Prince Charles was similarly endowed by Dundee on the occasion of his marriage to Princess Diana in 1981, although the castle then was painted from a different angle. The Duke of Edinburgh's private collection of paintings, gathered from Royal Scottish Academy exhibitions, includes Wellbank Farm, Carse of Gowrie. Several of Patrick's landscapes have also been reproduced on the personal Christmas cards of the Queen, Queen Mother, and other members of the Royal Family and have adorned countless company calendars. A McIntosh Patrick print is a favourite retiral gift and his pictures have been reproduced on biscuit tins and on table mats sold by Harrods.

TO SAY that McIntosh Patrick was a kenspeckle figure in the countryside around Dundee would be rather an understatement. He was almost part of the landscape itself, this familiar figure bent over an easel in a field or country lane, puffballs of white hair sprouting from the side of his head, constantly at work and constantly smoking. He was always a heroic smoker, first with cigarettes then later switching his allegiance to small cigars which he kept puffing away at almost to the day he died. There was an attempt made in his 90th year to stop the habit in the interests of achieving longevity but, employing all the wiles known to desperate men, he always managed somehow to get his hands on yet another packet of his favourite brand.

There were, of course, days when he would be absent on location due to weather being unfit for man or beast. On these occasions he would "edit", in the studio, the painting he was currently engaged on - tidying up work normally done in the evening. But being confined to barracks in this way during the day was a situation which turned him into a bear with a sore head. This became less of a problem, however, from 1984 onwards. In the winter of that year Patrick received a 'phone call from his friend Sir Norman Macfarlane, now Lord Macfarlane of Bearsden, a leading Scottish businessman who has had a long association with the Fine Art Society. When the artist complained during their conversation about being *stuck in the house* because of torrential rain his caller made an interesting suggestion. *Well, why don't you paint the scene in the studio itself and I'll buy the picture*, he said.

McIntosh Patrick grumbled that this wasn't quite his cup of tea but later that morning, having had second thoughts on the matter, decided to carry out the commission. The end product was a picture of consuming interest in which, with typical attention to detail, he 'repainted' all the other pictures which happened to be propped up in his studio at that time. This was the first of several pieces set in the studio, each one depicting pictures within a picture.

There was, however, one occasion when he was forced into a prolonged absence from outdoor work. This was caused by a perforated duodenal ulcer in the autumn of 1972 when he was rushed to hospital from his home one evening and underwent an emergency operation. He was critically ill for several days - the only time in his life he faced such a crisis - but his strong constitution pulled him through to an astonishing recovery at the age of 65. This may have been partly due to a recommendation that a modest intake of champagne would uplift his spirits during the flatter moments of his convalescence, medical advice which he duly followed. But he, himself, claimed that his restoration to full health had been due to a quite different type of 'remedy.'

Sitting at home one day shortly after leaving hospital, and feeling pretty awful, he decided to put on a scarf and sit outside in the garden. He used a Chinese jade brooch to pin the scarf in position – and from that moment began to feel progressively better. He had bought the brooch some time before in a Coupar Angus antique shop. The Chinese believe that jade confers longevity on those who wear it and with his recuperation now showing a marked improvement he, too, came to regard this piece of jewellery as a talisman. And from that day, every day, he wore it round his neck on a silver chain as in the frontispiece photgraph until he died 26 years later, aged 91. What is beyond conjecture, however, is the fact that he returned to painting with such renewed energy, no doubt thankful still to be alive, that he completed 40 watercolours in his first six months. Indeed, from then on McIntosh Patrick concentrated on water-colour, although his use of that medium was so powerful these pictures would often be mistaken for oils.

THE COURIER AND ADVERTISER, SATURDAY, OCTOBER 12, 1929.

BROUGHTY CASTLE    Specially Drawn By J. M'Intosh Patrick

*Beauty is something wonderful and strange*
*that the artist fashions*
*out of the chaos of the world*
*and the torment of his soul*

**My Studio**  *from a private collector/photograph The McManus Gallery*

THE COURIER AND ADVERTISER, SATURDAY MAY 24, 1930.

UNIVERSITY COLLEGE, DUNDEE

Specially Drawn by
J. M'INTOSH PATRICK

*A picture is not wrought by hand alone, good Padre, but by thought*

# The Teacher

MANY PEOPLE who are experts at what they do are unable, or sometimes unwilling, to share their knowledge or skills with others in a teaching capacity. McIntosh Patrick certainly did not belong to that school. His enthusiasm and ability in a classroom role became legendary. He was widely regarded as an outstanding - some would say an inspiring - teacher who encouraged and supported his pupils to a remarkable degree. He held a part-time lectureship at Dundee's College of Art from 1929 until a few years before he died in 1998.

And although he had a commitment to under-graduates for much of that time, it was the less formal weekly classes for adults which he took for fifty years from the end of the Second World War - really a form of further education - that were to spread his fame as a mentor among the general public. These sessions, held under the auspices of the Duncan of Jordanstone College of Art but without the rigour of examination or a demanding curriculum, were of two types: the indoor painting class held at the College on Saturday mornings and the outdoor summer sketching class which took place at rural locations on an evening during the week. All were invariably over-subscribed each year, attended by men and women from a' the airts and backgrounds, anxious to explore and develop their potential ability to paint and draw and to satisfy a creative need perhaps hitherto unexpressed. Several of these mature students were teachers themselves in other fields and so could recognise the outstanding qualities deployed by McIntosh Patrick when he took on the mantle of master.

His irrepressible enthusiasm for painting and drawing, and a conviction that it should always be *fun*, was the cornerstone of his teaching success. He installed a belief in everyone that they, too, could paint and draw and he allowed his pupils to develop their own style of painting. Although of the traditional school himself, he never imposed his beliefs on others. And he led them to understand that everything they created on paper or canvas was an original work of art never before executed in that particular way by anyone else and, therefore, was not to be destroyed. Above all, he made everyone feel they were somebody and in that context brushed his own achievements aside, determined that his fame and reputation would not intimidate those who were now his pupils.

He never rubbished anyone's work and, dire though it may have been, always found something good to say about it. He never advised anyone to give up and not come back. He was affable and pleasant and made a point of viewing every person's work at each session. He was never late for a class and worked

**Rapt attention at an indoor class**  *Mrs Isabella Ettle*

throughout each session, sometimes lasting four hours, without taking a break. *He was an inspiration to us all*, said one of his elderly pupils, *and would help us along by painting the odd bit of tree or dyke on our picture, showing us how it should be done.*

The outdoor class involved a certain degree of organisation, given that about thirty cars carrying nearly fifty pupils would be congregating at a spot in the country suitable for accommodating such numbers. Having arrived and spread themselves over a fairly wide area, McIntosh Patrick would then spend the next few hours trudging over fields, jumping streams, and climbing dykes, as he visited everyone in the class. If it was raining he would seek to shepherd his charges into a convenient shelter where he would proceed to give a demonstration in what then became a makeshift classroom. One of his pupils, Gordon Stewart, then deputy rector of Dundee High School, remembers such an occasion vividly: *Having got us into this barn he simply opened the door as wide as he could and proceeded to paint the view exactly as framed through the opening. It was amazing the way he did it. He could adapt to any situation. His expertise made painting look easy.*

Many of his amateur pupils went on to become competent artists, adding a new dimension to their lives, while several attained a professionalism which led to solo exhibitions and a keen demand for their work. Here are four of the former pupils who graduated with distinction from the McIntosh Patrick School of Painting:

Joe McIntyre was a 17-year-old apprentice iron-monger, with the dream of becoming an artist, when he joined one of the adult classes. Three years later he gained entry to Dundee College of Art as a full-time student, and three years after that graduated with his Diploma of Art. Joe has since been involved full-time in the field of art. He was curator of the Orchar Gallery in Broughty Ferry from 1969 until it closed in 1989. In 1972 he became a part-time lecturer at the Dundee Art College, a position he still holds today. As an artist who specialises in figurative city scenes in evening light his work is widely admired. *Jimmy Patrick was a huge influence in my life*, he says. *He helped so much in getting me where I am today.*

**Joe McIntyre** *and his painting* **Autumn Sunlight**

**Flowers & View from my window in Ibiza** *by Irene Furlong*

**Irene Furlong**

Irene Furlong came to Dundee in 1969 when her husband took up a hotel appointment in the city. The hotel's clientele included an artist whose work so stimulated her interest in painting that she joined the McIntosh Patrick class as a complete beginner. *I went along full of trepidation and to begin with I really struggled*, Irene recalls. *But Pat gave me so much encouragement I gradually found my feet. He opened my eyes to the world around me.* Irene went on to develop skills in pastels and oil, her work in flowers, figures, and portraiture attracting much attention. She spent ten years as a professional painter in Spain, specialising in murals and other decorative work with furnishings. She now has a studio at her home in Kippen, Stirlingshire.

Fred Livingstone was one of Patrick's prodigies. A hairdresser by profession, trading under the name of Fredericke, he had helped to introduce modern styling for women in the Dundee district in the late 1950's. But his name also became well-known through the painting skills he later developed as a pupil of the famous artist. His oil paintings set in fishing communities attracted much attention and were greatly sought after. His outstanding talent led him to spend several months each year painting in Normandy where his work was snapped up by various patrons, including a gallery in Paris.

**Self Portrait** and
**Ferryden, Montrose**
*by Fred Livingstone*

**Winter, Western Toronto** *by Cynthia Thulbourne*

**Cynthia Thulbourne**

When Cynthia Thulbourne settled in the Dundee area in 1976 she decided to develop her interest in painting by joining the famous adult class. In the years following she became almost a full-time artist through augmenting her class work by painting alongside McIntosh Patrick on location on a daily basis. Progress under his guidance brought her to exhibition level and *SOLD* tickets galore. As with all his pupils, her mentor taught her to observe the environment as she had never done before. *Mind you, I sometimes found it difficult concentrating on my work when out with Pat in the countryside with so many people stopping to speak to him. He, however, took it all in his stride, talking, painting and smoking all at the same time.* This was an act which fascinated many people.

THESE part-time adult classes were happy, almost social occasions with lots of banter, but they also involved a good deal of hard work. They still carry on to this day under another tutor and members continue to hold an annual exhibition of their work. The affection in which the artist was held by members of these classes was manifested in several ways. His birthday was invariably celebrated with a party and at the one held for his 88th anniversary Andrew Crawford, of Kirkcaldy, presented him with his portrait which he had painted from photographs. On his birthday three years before one of his other pupils had composed a poem of thanks, framing it within small pen sketches of the locations used by the outdoor class.

McIntosh Patrick's more academic aspect of teaching, and one which he relinquished in the late 1960's, was with under-graduates who were studying for their art diplomas. In this role also - a portfolio which took in painting, life drawing, composition, and art history - he displayed all the qualities of a fine lecturer; never aloof from his students, encouraging debate, and strong on fundamentals. His methods were sometimes rather unorthodox. He would, for example, often get down on his knees and, with a piece of chalk, demonstrate on the floor how to draw a dyke or a tree.

David Craig, who has his own studio in Dundee, was one of his students in the 1950's and fondly recalls the following incident: *Jimmy Patrick arrived in college one day with an oil painting still wet. He placed it on an easel and we all gathered round. 'Well, what are your comments?', he asked. We all stood around in silent awe, not wanting to speak out. I made a comment to the student next to me and on hearing my whisper McIntosh Patrick turned round and said, 'Well, speak up!'. I had no option*

**McIntosh Patrick** *by Andrew Crawford*

*but to give vent to my feelings about his superb painting of the Sidlaw Slate Quarries with its lovely background going into the distance, but spoiled in my opinion by a small group of gypsies and a tent which distracted me from a fine piece of composition.*

*My remark was followed by complete silence. For a few minutes no-one dared speak. Then Jimmy produced a penknife and opened the blade. I thought he was going to slash my canvas and say start again, but to everyone's surprise he went to his own canvas and scraped out the gypsies then, borrowing a brush and palette, he painted over the scrape marks. He then stood back and said: 'That's better. Let that be a lesson. No matter how good you think you are someone can at times improve your painting by a casual remark. Just listen, reassess, and don't be afraid to make changes if you think it is necessary.'* Indeed, he was prone to asking someone watching him paint, very often a non-artist, whether they thought he should include a certain item in his picture. On these occasions the person being consulted would be flattered to death.

Many of the under-graduate sessions were enlivened by fierce arguments between McIntosh Patrick and his friendly rival, Alberto Morrocco, who was then head of the School of Painting. While the class looked on in awe the two men would cross swords over the merits of their respective painting styles and techniques. Alberto, a distinguished artist in his own right, was a modernist who failed to see the need for the meticulous detail and realism practiced by Patrick. Patrick, on the other hand, couldn't understand why many of Morrocco's compositions and figures were not exactly what the eye was seeing. As Alberto said years later: *Jimmy would be on the floor measuring things out with a bit of string to prove his style of painting and I would be saying that I wouldn't mind*

*students painting inaccurately if they captured the spirit of their subject. But he was a stickler for accuracy. The students must often have wondered what was going on.*

McINTOSH PATRICK was a very tolerant man free from prejudice, and this applied to his views and opinions on art. He believed in individual expression when it came to painting and drawing, although it must be said he was often less enthusiastic about the type of art which did not relate to the environment as he knew it. *If you know the world is round,* he would say, *you couldn't paint it as if it were flat... If anything is basic to your understanding then it comes out in what you're painting. It has always puzzled me why Picasso could paint women with three eyes. I don't object to that. It's simply that I don't understand why he should think of it.*

On one memorable occasion when asked what he thought of the paintings in a modern exhibition he had just visited, Patrick replied: *Very interesting - but it's a pity the artist gave up just when things were starting to get difficult.*

Speaking on a television programme in 1978, he laid out his own stall in this matter in his usual stimulating manner: *I find that when I see a great many modern pictures the artist seems to set the spectator a kind of puzzle. He doesn't seem clear in his own mind, and I'm sure the spectator gets still less from it. But I think there is abroad a kind of feeling that originality is tremendously important. At all expense you must be original. Now, the old masters, and other artists in the past, have never thought in this way at all.*

*If you were alive in the 15th and 16th centuries and someone asked you to paint Madonna and Child you wouldn't say 'Oh, I'm not painting Madonna and Child. Botticelli did one last week'. You would be quite happy to have your attempt at Madonna and Child regarded as the effort of someone who wanted to paint it and trust that your own individuality, your own colour sense and sense of proportion, will come through and people would know that yours is not a Botticelli but is a Leonardo or a Michelangelo or one of the other great artists of the 16th century. The same in Chinese art which I admire enormously. You can become famous in China by being good at imitating the style of an earlier artist, with just a little bit of your own personality coming through.* (He was also attracted to Chinese art because he found it good-natured and amusing; hardly ever cruel, with even the depiction of wild animals manifesting a certain gentleness).

*I am quite sure that a great many young artists today bang up against a stone wall by thinking it is absolutely important to think of a subject, new kinds of subjects, new things to say. I think they are encouraged to do so by critics and so on, whereas in actual fact they would have happy lives, successful lives, if they used their talents in just the most direct way; not listening to critics and trying to knock people over backwards at exhibitions and so on, but by going back to first principles and going back to Nature and being themselves and not trying to be extrovert and worrying all the time about the sensation they are going to be in exhibitions.*

These observations are not difficult to understand in one whose sense of traditionalism and realism was deeply ingrained. Here was a man, as Alberto Morrocco had pointed out, whose obsession with detail would lead him to lay his canvas on the floor at the sketching stage of a picture and measure different aspects of the composition for distance, height, and size with bits of string. Before painting a roof or a dyke on location he would actually count the tiles and make a tally of the stones. And at various stages of the work taking shape on the easel he would often turn his back to the canvas and view his picture through a

**The Famous Signature
signed backwards**
*see story on page 11 column 2*

hand mirror. This allowed him to see his painting in reverse and for a moment this was like seeing it for the first time. Faults to which his eye may have been accustomed would immediately become apparent. His addiction to accuracy was typically demonstrated when he was painting a Dundee church and was anxious to capture the sunlight striking the spire at a precise angle. This could only be achieved at a certain time of day, and at the time of year he was working on the picture this effect was only available at 6.30 in the morning. But he was duly in position long before others were out of bed. On the other hand, he would often insert or remove a detail from a landscape, or perhaps move a feature to a different position, if he felt it would enhance the painting without under-mining the overall integrity of the composition.

THE COURIER AND ADVERTISER, SATURDAY, JANUARY 25, 1930.

## GLAMIS CASTLE  ∴

Specially Drawn by J. M'Intosh Patrick

*A subject he would return to in later years but with brush and palette*

Patrick would sometimes even lapse into a favourite piece of verse when discussing the unusual and off-beat in art:

> The artist and his luckless wife,
> They lead a horrid, haunted life,
> Surrounded by the things he's made,
> Which are not wanted by the trade.
> The artist is an awful man,
> He doesn't do the things he can.
> He does the things he cannot do,
> And we attend the private view.
> He tampers with the works of God,
> And makes them look uncommon odd.

He would then say: *I don't see the point of devoting your whole life to doing something without it meaning something to someone else.* Patrick was certainly intrigued by the distorted images created by many artists in order to produce a strong emotional effect without undermining the overall integrity of the composition. Referring to the presence of storms in some of these paintings he would tell the story of King George VI attending an exhibition one year at Windsor and later saying to the artist: *I enjoyed your pictures, but what a pity you had such bad weather.*

As artist and teacher, however, he took the broad view on the matter of style. He knew the way he wanted to paint. It was up to others to take that decision for themselves and he respected the integrity of those who painted with a different brush. He was a man for all seasons.

---

*Everything that man esteems*
*Endures a moment or a day*
*Loves pleasure drives his love away*
*The painters brush consumes his dreams*

---

# The Man

THEY SAY that the real test of a person's class is the way they treat others who cannot possibly do them any good. If that is so, then McIntosh Patrick was one of the classiest persons you could ever hope to meet. His capacity for friendship was astonishing. Strangers coming to the door seeking advice about their work, or simply anxious to make his acquaintance, would likely be invited in, shown round the studio with an up-date on his latest painting, and then probably offered a cup of tea. He had time for everyone.

For those who wished to paint alongside him on location there was rarely ever a problem. There was no side to the man, and he gave short shrift to prima-donnas. Robert Louden, a civil servant who lives in Currie, Midlothian, and is himself a successful artist, flourished under Patrick's friendship and teaching and is one of his most fervent admirers. He first spotted his work at the Royal Scottish Academy in 1966 and met him four years later following an exhibition in Edinburgh. That was the start of a long association which took Bob to Dundee at least once a year to join his idol on location with his easel. *He had no need to befriend me at all,* says Bob. *I was just another artist, but he treated me as an equal and taught me a great deal about various aspects of painting and drawing.*

On one occasion McIntosh Patrick suggested they carry out a painting experiment in which they would exchange spectacles and then paint the same view as seen through the other person's glasses. *This will lead to a form of impressionism rather than a detailed work*, said the maestro with a twinkle in his eye. *He was right*, Bob recalls with a laugh. *The results were most interesting! But this was typical of the man's sense of fun. I regard myself as very lucky to have known him.*

Those who came upon him painting in the countryside were also guaranteed a friendly welcome. John Nicholson and his wife, who live in Blairgowrie, were out cycling one spring day in 1995 when they spotted the artist painting in the village of Kettins . He chatted to them for some time and let slip that he was 88 that very day. The following morning Mr Nicholson, a keen amateur painter, loaded ten of his pictures into the back of his car and returned to Kettins. He had decided to take the plunge and ask McIntosh Patrick to assess his work: *Much to my relief he agreed right away, telling me to arrange my paintings against the side of the car. Then, sitting in a deck chair, he proceeded to go over them one by one. I shall always remember how helpful and gracious he was.*

The warmth of his personality, however, was extended to all who had contact with him in circles far beyond the fraternity of artists. As a schoolboy, Alistair Craig's evening newspaper round took in McIntosh

Patrick's house in Magdalen Yard Road: *He invited me into his home on a number of occasions and it always seemed to be full of the most exotic people having interminable discussions about life, the universe, and everything. It was only too easy for me to join in and get caught up, which infuriated many other customers on my round. He took me into the studio, too, sometimes, showing me works in progress and giving the odd demonstration of artistic technique.*

*When I was unwell at any time my brother and sister covered my paper round for me and they both struck up the same rapport with him, particularly my sister. Mr Patrick lived near the end of her route and by the time she got there he was at the gate and would finish the round with her, walking arm in arm along the road. A true gentleman, he always saw her to the door and safely inside. He was a magic man, in the true sense of the word. He was one of the people who helped to open up the world for my sister, my brother and myself. He will never be forgotten.*

Painting, like writing, can be a lonely business, but McIntosh Patrick was never a loner. On the contrary, he was a most sociable man and loved the company of others as he loved his own family. He generated a constant flow of conversation and had very definite opinions on whatever subject was being discussed. He was never dull. When he spoke it was not a case of separating the wheat from the chaff, but separating the wheat from the wheat. Before the war his studio was a meeting place for fellow artists debating matters of the day, with Patrick joining in as he worked away on his latest painting. At The Shrubbery, too, there were regular evenings of heated discussion, broken only by the host displaying his virtuosity at the piano with a sonata or a Scottish country dance number. James Reville, one of his distinguished contemporaries, summed up this side of him thus in a magazine article written while his friend was still alive:

Wherever Patrick is, there is talk. The spate of words that has issued from his lips is not the least of his output. He talks as easily as most people breathe and he can talk as he works and even as he listens. It has not been unknown for a chance encounter at 10pm on a fine summer's evening to develop into a four hour conversation, the participants finding their way home at 2am 'and no regrets'. His talk is forthright, forceful and assertive. He is very good at votes of thanks. Many chairmen must have been grateful to him for his unfailing expertness and for the discussions started by him at question time.

Andrew, his son, tells of late nights cornered by his father in conversation: *At two in the morning I would tell him I was dead beat and would have to go to bed. At 7.30 the next morning the dog would come in and nudge me awake. Then a voice would say: 'I'm sorry about that. Now, as I was saying to you last night….*

IT IS but a short step from friendliness to helpfulness and so it comes as no surprise to learn that the artist contributed much to good causes in the way of fund-raising pictures and prints. In 1987, for example, he was appalled to learn that the Victorian bandstand on Magdalen Green in front of his house was in danger of being demolished because it had been allowed to fall into a state of disrepair. He said: *I see the bandstand and the rail bridge as going together. Both are fine examples of Victorian ironwork. You couldn't say there were any frills about the bridge. Maybe they built the bandstand to show what they could really do. Walking along of an evening and seeing the bandstand in a sunset, there are connotations of empire - reflecting the kind of buildings the Victorians saw in India at the time. The bandstand so strongly suggests its period, and the days have surely been long gone when Victorian art was despised. It's part of our history, this bandstand, something that belongs not just to us but to our children as well. How anyone could contemplate taking it down…well, I just don't know.*

**The Victorian Bandstand on Magdalen Green** *from a print by Fraser & Sons, Dundee*

At that point he agreed to paint a picture of the bandstand in its landscape setting by the river, the proceeds from which, along with a portion of the print sales, to be given to the restoration fund. The painting fetched £5000 at auction and the bandstand was duly refurbished in time for its centenary in 1990. A dedication service the following year was attended by the Queen Mother. McIntosh Patrick also gave generously of his time away from the easel, presenting slide shows of his work at countless functions until well into his eighties and always being available for school talks, prize-givings, exhibition openings and tree plantings.

He was also a witty man who enjoyed telling funny stories, even if they were at his own expense. There was the time he was painting at a farm on the outskirts of Dundee when the farmer engaged him in conversation. After a few minutes it was obvious the man had no idea who the artist was. *You don't know me?*, Patrick asked, unable to conceal surprise that his celebrity status had failed to penetrate this corner of the countryside. This was at the time of his 80th birthday retrospective exhibition, an event being heralded all over Dundee by street banners and posters bearing his name. *Canna say a' do*, replied the farmer, pushing back his bonnet and scratching his head in perplexity. Then he added: *Mind you, a' wid o' kent ye fine if ye had been a doo fancier.*

But when it came to humour Pat would enjoy nothing more than going through his collection of Macdonald cartoons which at one time were great favourites in the Weekly News. He would often pore over them in great spasms of laughter, despite having studied these joke drawings countless times before. He would even delight in telling the story lines without producing the cartoons at all. *Remember that one?*, he

"Ye've got yer boat upside doon, Mac!"

would say from the depths of his favourite armchair in his living room, and then go on to tell you of the big, fat domineering woman watching her husband floundering about in the harbour having fallen in. *Are ye no' goin' tae call for help?*, asks the shocked wee man at her side. *Aye, but eh'll gie him a few mair minutes yet.*

He also chuckled when reminiscing about the commission he was given in 1958 to paint a cow, a prize Belted Galloway owned by Lord David Stuart, of Mochrum Castle, Port William, Wigtownshire. It was not an easy task. Slaethorn was a restless 'sitter' to put it mildly, continually twisting and turning on the end of a rope held by the herdsman as she kept an eye on her new bull calf. *It was all very difficult*, said the artist rather ruefully. *I had to keep moving my easel about, swivelling 90 degrees at times to make sure I had the animal in the right position. I was trying to paint the cow accurately...as a cow. But Lord David and the herdsman were obviously seeing it in a different way and so they kept me right on certain technical points. I also brought the castle into the background, giving an interesting picture at the end of the day.*

But his most unusual commission was the one involving the portrait of Lady Lyell of Kinnordy, whose husband, Lord Lyell, posthumous winner of the V.C., had been painted by Patrick at the outset of the Second World War. In 1946 he had then started on a portrait of Lord Lyell's widow, although the final sittings could not be fitted in at the time and the unfinished picture was forgotten about until 24 years later when it was found languishing in a store-room at Kinnordy. Lady Lyell's son insisted on the portrait being completed and so Patrick went back to the big house where his subject donned the same dress she had previously worn and stood in the same position at the bottom of the carved staircase. *It was a very curious experience*, the artist said later. *When I resumed the portrait all the conversations Lady Lyell and I had were about that period of time when I first started the picture. It was if we had both stepped back into the past.*

McIntosh Patrick was equally at home in cottage or castle. Rubbing shoulders with the hoi polloi came as easily to him as consorting with the aristocracy. Mary, Countess of Strathmore, has fond memories of the artist when he painted her portrait at Glamis Castle in 1979, several years after her late husband succeeded to the title. *It was decided that I should sit in the billiard room for the painting because it was north facing and therefore provided an even light*, she recalls. *However, at that time of year the castle was still open to the public and the billiard room was part of the tour. So there we were, artist and subject, being scrutinised by all these visitors, many of whom thought I was a wax model, so still did I have to sit. Anyway, it was good fun and Dr Patrick wasn't in the slightest bit put out.*

These visits to the castle by the artist were keenly anticipated by the Strathmore children who would join him and their mother for lunch during which

*With his painting of Lady Lyell*

Patrick would keep everyone highly entertained by quoting the work of P. G. Wodehouse at great length. *He could reel off page after page from various books by the author - his memory was quite astonishing*, says the mother of the present Earl. *The children loved his company. He was so good at treating them as adults.*

When Prince Andrew married Sarah Ferguson in 1986, Lord and Lady Strathmore commissioned Dr Patrick to paint a picture of Glamis Castle as a wedding present for the couple. This was the third time he had tackled this subject for the purpose of a royal wedding gift (Princess Margaret and Prince Charles being previous recipients) and, as on the previous occasions, he located his easel in a different part of the grounds.

McINTOSH PATRICK'S 'open door' policy extended to all sections of the media, and throughout his life he enjoyed a mutually beneficial relationship with all those involved in news, features and documentaries. The result was that he possibly received greater coverage than any other Scottish artist of his time, perhaps even for all time. He had an eloquence of expression which matched that of his painting, conveyed in the same engaging style that caught the attention and imagination of the public. He was also a past master in describing his thoughts and feelings in a nut-shell, what today is called a soundbite. He wasn't in the slightest bit intimidated by cameras or microphones and was a genuinely natural performer. In other words, he was extremely good copy. And, although never bragging about his work, he was never unduly modest either and, therefore, enjoyed the publicity.

His most successful television documentary was possibly the one filmed by BBC Scotland and transmitted on a Sunday evening in January, 1978, under the title 'Seeing is Believing.' The programme was partly filmed in his wonderful city garden at the back of The Shrubbery and gave him the perfect platform to voice his views on nature, man, and the environment. His sincerity, simplicity and sheer common sense came shining through to such an extent that he was overwhelmed by viewers' letters and 'phone calls, adding a further battalion of admirers to his already considerable army of followers.

Over the years he had explained, as he did again on the programme, that his garden was largely a wild and natural creation, many of the plants having grown from seeds dropped by birds or blown in by the wind. People, he said, were often obsessed with weeding and in the course of doing so were throwing away lots of interesting little plants. *Many folk do too much gardening,* he declared, giving hope to thousands of husbands being harassed into action by nagging wives. *Gardening should go along with nature.* He disliked passion for tidiness in the garden and although a certain amount of pruning was necessary, he deplored wholesale cutting back. *Have things in the garden that look happy,* he urged. *If plants are miserable you finish up with a hospital for unhappy plants. Nature wants to be lush. Gardens should be as restful as possible.*

As he walked through the garden, where his outdoor sketching class was sometimes held, he would tell you: *I don't necessarily want to say that plants know what's happening to them, but look at these rowan trees. They're all very straight, but if this branch had grown in a natural direction it would have been sawn off because it would have been an obstruction. Instead, it has wound itself round the tree as if it knew that if it was going to survive it had to do that. I suppose there is another explanation, but this one suits me......And look at this cotoneaster growing from under the paving stone. My wife suggested one day that I pull it out before it caught on people's clothes. I didn't do it, and look what's happened. That other flower has reached out from the side and pulled it back.*

*When you spend as much time as me out of doors studying nature you get to believe that everything, this life force in*

**Garden Painting 1979**   *Dundee Arts and Heritage, McManus Gallery*

*plants and animals and human beings, is very important, and you get the idea that you should destroy as little as possible of what's alive. I am silly enough to chase flies out of the car because I don't want to take them away from their friends. I am sentimental enough not to look at a bird's nest to see how many eggs there are because I believe that birds deserve their own privacy. If I find slugs on a lettuce in the kitchen I return them carefully to the garden. I do honestly believe that anything alive should be treated with respect. People may think this is all very silly, but if young folk were to see more of this there would be less vandalism. They would come to respect young trees and things.*

Ironically, however, it was the darker side of nature which destroyed the pride and joy of his garden, an 80-foot high eucalyptus tree with a vast spread of branches which had become a well-known landmark within the inner city. He had planted it in 1947 as a two-inch potted sprig. Now, with its beautiful blue-green foliage, it towered over everything and had featured in several paintings. The tree was a constant source of pleasure to its keeper - until a gale blew it down in January, 1984. For McIntosh Patrick this was rather like the loss of a close friend and the passing of the tree was duly reported across four columns in the local press. It was an obituary notice allocated the space normally reserved for the death of a local dignitary.

Switching to the environment, and still speaking at the time of the programme in 1979, he said there were tremendous economic pressures on architects and town planners but he sometimes felt that, although they claimed to marry up the new to the old, new buildings still stuck out like a sore thumb, resembling car batteries standing on end. He thought that architects, like everyone else, were bitten by the bug that everything had to be completely new. Schools which had been happy places for a long time had to be

pulled down and replaced by buildings which had so much glass they blinded the pupils and cost a fortune to keep clean: *I just feel that everyone is rushing forward in a crazy sort of way. Everything is old hat. I don't find this in my own work. Ordinary persons interested in paintings don't crave for new things at all. People still want prints of pictures I did forty years ago. But no sooner do you have a television set nowadays when someone is saying you need a new one. You can't go for a walk in the country but you have to pull a boat behind your car. You can't go for a walk in the snow without skis, and so on.*

McIntosh Patrick would also speak about a thunderstorm in which lightning had struck one of the piers of the old Gothic gateway to the Western Cemetery in Dundee. The top of the column had been wrenched round and, although in his opinion nothing had really been damaged, workmen on ladders had used crow bars to send the displaced blocks of stone smashing to the pavement. He had seen this happen: *As each section came down pupils from a nearby school were cheering. I attempted to stop this vandalism but failed. Everything could have been restored by a mason if only some thought had been given to the matter.* He spoke about the enormous care that had been put into the design of the gateway, with each of the panels carrying biblical texts. He then quoted from one of the panels:

The days of our years are three score years and ten; and if by reason of strength they are four score years, yet is there strength, labour and sorrow; for it is soon cut off and we fly away. So teach us to number our days that we may apply our hearts unto wisdom. For what is your life? It is ever a vapour that appeareth for a little time, and then vanisheth away. Seek ye first the Kingdom of God, and His right-eousness, and all these things shall be added unto you.

He said that the media led us to believe the world was a miserable place full of unhappy and frustrated people, that we had become a nation of pill takers and that everyone's nerves were on edge. To counteract this, he thought we should teach people at a very young age that they had been born into a beautiful world. *The ugly bits in it are the bits we did and we have made and most of it is unnecessary. It's not just a case of money and expense. It's a case of imagination and sensitivity. Half the places that look so hideous could be cleared up quite easily.*

Turning to personal relationships, he said he was very fond of dogs and children and got on well with both, to the extent that he tended to know the names of dogs without knowing the names of the owners. Any time he whistled to a dog it would come to him with its tail wagging and tongue hanging out in appreciation of being spoken to. It was the same with children. Speak to them, he said, as you would to an adult, but about things within their own experience, and they would respond. As for striking a chord with other people, he found that if he said 'Good morning' to someone who didn't know him they tended to fall over backwards with astonishment.

He would then add: *If you are frightened to smile to someone in case they think you are trying to get off with them or that you want to borrow a cigarette then, of course, you won't smile. But if you are confident enough in yourself you can afford to do it. If people tried to be more friendly with each other without being false about it, instead of scowling as if each other wasn't there, everyone would be much happier.* McIntosh Patrick was in love with life. He once said: *The world is a wonderful place. I simply can't get enough of it.*

James and Janet Patrick on their Golden Wedding

BEARING in mind his extrovert nature, it is not surprising that the McIntosh Patrick household inevitably centred round the artist himself. After a day normally spent painting in solitary confinement he was not the sort of person who came home from work to sit quietly by the fireside, listening dutifully to family gossip. Although a home-bird he was not a domesticated animal. He liked to be the person who made things happen, calling the tune and revelling in the attention of others, whether it was being danced upon him by his own family or by the steady stream of admirers who crossed the threshold. When you ask Andrew, his son, if he enjoyed a normal family life, he replies perceptively, if not informatively: *I don't know. It was the only one I knew. We certainly discussed art as other families might discuss football.*

His father also liked to be to the fore on social occasions, both at home and away, and could be counted on to grab more than his fair share of the conversation, albeit in a most invigorating fashion, brushing aside interruptions and surging on in a flood of opinionated thought. Pre-dinner talk would very often prevent other guests from reaching the table while the meal was still hot and there was at least one hostess who reverted to cold dishes when Patrick was coming to the house. Even his own grandchildren found it difficult getting a word in edgeways and during one family meal it was jokingly suggested to them that they might have more success in speaking to their grandfather if they went to the kiosk at the end of the road and 'phoned him up! It was indeed fortunate that Janet, his wife, was a tolerant, patient and supportive person. She was also a home-loving and devoted mother and her death in July, 1983, only a week after celebrating her golden wedding, was much mourned.

**Ann Hunter** *and her painting* **Casa San Martino, Asolo** *(opposite)*

The Patrick dynasty is headed up today by his son Andrew and daughter Ann. Ann, born in 1937, took her Diploma of Art at Dundee in 1959 and has been a successful profess-ional painter ever since, developing her own style in executing a wide variety of subjects from flowers and fruit to landscapes and portraits. She is of a much more retiring nature than her father, although still willing to speak of her days as a young girl interested in still life painting involving fruit. Very often she would finish up eating the pears and apples instead of using them as subject matter! Ann is married to Dick Hunter, also an artist, who was a full-time lecturer at Dundee College of Art for 33 years. Their three children are all engaged in various aspects of art, architecture and design.

Andrew was born in 1934 and is unmarried. Miraculously it might be thought due to his family background, he has never been a "hands on" person in art. Ask him why and he replies rather curtly: *Because I was never any good at it.* He then explains: *my art mark at school was only around 30%. When father saw this on my report card he pondered for a few seconds before saying, 'Well, I don't suppose even Michelangelo would get 100%'.* Andrew, however, is one of Britain's leading art dealers and is the managing director of the prestigious Fine Art Society in London.

His own collection of paintings and objects d'art is eclectic and much admired. He possesses the works of many artists and is particularly fond of paintings by Paul Maitland who moved in the same circle as the celebrated Whistler. *Maitland speaks to you if you're in the right mood*, he says. He will then direct your gaze to Maitland's painting of a wood in Kensington Gardens and maintain that each time you look at it more people seem to be emerging from behind the trees. *It's a kind of magic*, he claims. He also has a fine range of Japanese prints, rare furniture by Edward Godwin, and embroideries from Persia. He has the biggest private collection of ceramics and metalwork by Christopher Dresser.

Andrew is also very fond of camels through his visits to North Africa and has them modelled in bronze, terracotta, and wood, transformed into egg cups and painted on to plates. A picture postcard of one camel carries the health warning: 'Never take a drag from the wrong end of a camel.' In the flat prior to the one he now occupies, room space was so restricted that not only was every inch of wall occupied by pictures and other works of art, but he

**Andrew Patrick**

also had them hanging on the backs of doors – and even pinned to the ceiling. This latter innovation was the brainchild of a dentist who wished to give his patients pretty pictures to look at as they lay back in his chair. It is not surprising that Andrew Patrick is an avid collector, given his expertise as an art dealer.

This appreciation of art is obviously inherited from his father who also liked to be surrounded by the work of other artists and outstanding craftsmen. Indeed, crossing the threshold of The Shrubbery was rather like entering a treasure house of paintings, period furniture and furnishings, Chinese soapstone carvings and other Oriental pieces, rare porcelain, fine rugs and carpets, and a wide range of European and Oriental ceramics and works of art. The walls and display cabinets offered many things of beauty. McIntosh Patrick spent much time browsing in antique shops.

When he died the Patrick Collection, comprising 300 lots, was auctioned off by Christie's in Glasgow and fetched a total of almost £300,000.

**A Wood in Kensington Gardens** *by Paul Maitland*

**In the Living Room of The Shrubbery** *Courtesy of DC Thomson & Co Ltd, Dundee*

# The Accolades

ALTHOUGH McIntosh Patrick never sought any honours or tributes, or any form of public acclaim, his celebrity status was constantly recognised at academic and civic level. From the time he was elected an Associate of the Royal Society of Painter-Etchers and Engravers at the age of only 25 in 1932, he was decorated on many occasions.

In 1949 he was elected an Associate of the Royal Scottish Academy and a member of the Royal Institute of Oil Painters. In 1957 he was made a full member of the RSA, although much earlier had narrowly missed out on election to the Royal Academy. In 1986 he was awarded an Honorary Fellowship of the Duncan of Jordanstone College of Art (the successor of Dundee College of Art) and eight years later, at the age of 87, was similarly honoured by his alma mater, the Glasgow School of Art, at which time he was their oldest working graduate. At the highest academic level he received an Honorary Doctorate of Laws from the University of Dundee in 1973 and in 1995 was capped with an Honorary Doctorate of Arts by the University of Abertay, Dundee.

**1973,** *Receiving his Doctorate from Her Majesty Queen Elizabeth the Queen Mother, Chancellor of Dundee University*

THE DUNDEE COURIER

All this he took in his stride in his usual unassuming manner, once observing that although he got letters from lots of people who thought he was one of the best landscape painters Scotland had ever produced, there were just as many others who thought he 'couldn't paint for toffee.' Being human, however, he didn't exactly enjoy rejection. When the Royal Glasgow Institute of the Fine Arts turned down one of his watercolours for their 1989 annual exhibition he commented: *I'm amused - although I won't be sending to them again.*

Exhibitions of his work were also a manifestation of the high regard in which he was held and these were a recurring theme in the arts calendar. The consistency of his popularity was such that when Dundee Art Galleries staged its first major McIntosh Patrick exhibition in 1967, 30,000 people flocked to the venue. At the time of his next major retrospective 20 years later to mark his 80th birthday in 1987, there had been no waning of interest - indeed the attendance of 45,000 over six weeks at the same gallery constituted a record for a Dundee exhibition. Milling crowds, including visitors world-wide, swamped the event and besieged the artist for autographs whenever he appeared on the scene. The work, spanning 65 years, had been gathered in from other galleries, private collectors, and members of the Royal Family. After it was all over the organiser Clara

*A warm word for everyone viewing the 80th Birthday exhibition in McManus Gallery*

**94** *The Accolades*

Young reported: *On the last day with 3,400 visitors we were going like a fair. The artist was there for hours cheerfully signing catalogues. The gallery shop was mobbed. The whole exhibition made a profit and we had to write to the Scottish Arts Council to say, 'We don't need your grant - thanks all the same.'*

The collection was later transferred to Aberdeen and Liverpool where attendances brought the total number of visitors at the three venues to over 100,000. Indeed, more people turned up at Aberdeen Art gallery than at any other exhibition in the city for many years, even those including the works of Turner and Leonardo da Vinci. At the Walker Art Gallery in Liverpool the exhibition literature described Patrick as *Dundee's L.S.Lowry* and went on:

> As with Lowry, Patrick appears content to explore and re-explore places close at hand - familiar to him, perhaps, but their invariable human associations always changing – taking no account of artistic fashion or critical fortune but remaining faithful to his fixed and individual point of view.

Ten years later, his 90th birthday tribute took the form of three exhibitions, two in Dundee and one at The Scottish National Gallery of Modern Art in Edinburgh. Reviewing these events, art critic Duncan Macmillan, writing in the Scotsman, said:

> He is an artist in the very best academic tradition. What he does well, he does supremely well. And he has recorded something essential about our landscape, for in his life-time the countryside he has painted has changed dramatically. Machines have replaced people, but this only makes his best pictures more precious. We owe him thanks and wish him many happy returns.

He also exhibited at the Royal Scottish Academy from the age of 19 until the year before he died in 1998 and was regularly hung at the Royal Academy in London until 1962 at which point he decided to

*The cake on the 90th Birthday.*
*The artist surrounded by family, including Andrew and Ann and friends including Sandy and Morag Saddler*

concentrate on the Scottish gallery scene. His paintings are, of course, on permanent exhibition at countless galleries in this country and abroad. However, being able to pop into a gallery to admire a certain artist's work is not always convenient. Better still if you can have these pictures hanging on your own walls at home.

The problem with that, of course, is the prohibitive cost of original paintings for the popular market. This, however, has been overcome through the tremendous growth in reproductions, the availability of high quality prints at affordable prices within the reach of the average person. The popularity of McIntosh Patrick's paintings - the *People's Artist* - made his work a natural target for this wider circulation and well over fifty of his original pictures, possibly more than any other Scottish artist, have so far been reproduced in highly successful editions. Patrick's work, including the Four Seasons, first went into print before the second world war and this trend continued with other paintings in later years through a variety of mainly English publishers including Dickens, Cavendish, Medici and, more recently, Rosenstiel's, of London. Then Fraser & Son of Dundee, the well-known art dealers, with whom the artist had a close business and personal relationship, decided to enter the reproduction market with Patrick's work in 1979 by producing **Dundee from Carse of Gowrie** as their first signed limited edition, since when they have brought out another thirteen of his paintings in print form at regular intervals. But they have not had the field to themselves.

In 1978 Alf Paladini, also of Dundee, realised his dream of opening his own gallery by launching such an enterprise in Broughty Ferry under the name of Eduardo Alessandro Studios. Five years later, having witnessed the demand for the artist's work, Mr Paladini decided that he, too, would get into the print business. He chose Patrick's widely-acclaimed painting, **Tay Bridge from my Studio Window**, with which to make his debut. It was a brilliant choice. The edition came off the presses in the run up to Christmas that year, 1983, and was a best seller from the word go, despite it having been printed by a previous owner of the original painting many years before. It seemed that every second person in Dundee wanted a copy of the Tay Bridge print and hundreds have since gone abroad to expatriates all over the world, reproductions now to be found in houses as far apart as Newfoundland and New Zealand. With this particular print being an unlimited, or open, edition it is still a popular seller today, making it a juicy dripping roast in the reproduction industry.

Sandro Paladini, the son of Alf and a partner in what is now the biggest independent gallery in the East of Scotland, enthusiastically describes the Tay Bridge painting as McIntosh Patrick's 'Mona Lisa.' He makes no secret of the fact that this initial reproduction boosted the fortunes of his own gallery and had encouraged his firm to put a further 27 Patrick paintings into print form so far. Says Sandro Paladini: *The commercial success of the Patrick prints has also allowed us to invest in the work of other Scottish artists in a way which might not have been possible otherwise.* All this increased activity in reproducing Patrick's paintings when the artist was in his mid-70's added up to circulation on an impressive scale, conferring almost cult status on the artist at an international level at a time of life when he could not have expected to be spending hours, sometimes days, signing thousands of prints.

At auctions, too, and at selling exhibitions, his

**Carse of Gowrie** 1937 *Fine Art Society Ltd.*

reputation has always been widely acknowledged in the enhanced prices which his work consistently commands on an upward scale, sometimes being bought unseen. As the auctioneer's hammer heralds yet another record figure there is much comparison with original values, no more so than in April, 1999, when Sotheby's disposed of a McIntosh Patrick painting of the **Carse of Gowrie** for £54,300, a record price so far at auction for a picture which had earned the artist £125 in 1937. (Illustrated on previous page). Several of his signed prints are now valued at over £700 and will no doubt soon break the thousand pound barrier.

Considering the sheer volume of his output, an estimated 2,500 works, quite a number of his paintings have re-entered the market and, of course, will always do so. When they did appear in salerooms during his lifetime he was constantly asked how he reacted to the fortunes being pocketed by others for pictures he had originally sold at what now looked like peppercorn prices. On these occasions he would simply shrug his shoulders and say he was flattered his work was sufficiently highly thought of that people were prepared to dig so deeply into their pockets to acquire it, and having done so would be likely to look after these pictures. He himself had felt well enough paid at the time for what he had done.

When a pupil at an adult class questioned him about one particular painting which had changed hands for £15,000, he remarked: *Yes, wasn't that good? But you know I was well pleased when I sold it for £200. That kept my wife and family fed at that time for a month.* Very often, however, he would show his irritation when taxed on the subject. *Don't talk to me about money*, he told one reporter. *I can't be doing with this money business. I sell my pictures by the square inch and I put everything I can into them. Some artists get the same prices as I do with pictures they've painted between lunch and dinner, but my kind of pictures take time because they are usually complicated and highly finished.* The fact was that Patrick was never at home with balance sheets and cash flow and, by his own admission, would have earned a good deal more had he exercised greater commercial acumen. There was the time when he was approached by two young admirers, not long left school, who said they would treasure one of his paintings but could only afford to pay him £50 between them. Without hesitation he said he would paint them a picture to meet that price – and did so.

THERE were many other laurels bestowed on McIntosh Patrick over the years, several at grass-roots level which he treated with the same sense of humility as he regarded those from more elevated quarters. In 1979 one of his greatest admirers, Ernest Massie, of Dundee, well-known for his versifying, was moved to write a ten-verse poem in tribute to the artist. Before presenting it to him framed at an outdoor class in The Shrubbery garden, Mr Massie read his eulogy aloud to the gathering of artists. The final verse ran:

> There's so much that can be said, by old friends and those anew,
> But our thoughts are all the same, it's a pleasure knowing you.
> So enjoy the passing years, and the happiness they bring,
> Best of luck to you and yours, many thanks for everything.

Much later on it was the turn of Ron Gonella, one of Scotland's leading fiddlers, to show his appreciation in the form of a specially-composed tune, 'The McIntosh Patrick March,' which was performed in the Caird Hall by the Dundee Strathspey and Reel

**1992**
*visiting*
*The Broons in*
*The Sunday Post*
*see page 101*

**OBE Investiture at the City Chambers 1997.**
*left to right:* Elliot, Lord Provost Mervyn Rolfe, artist with Liberty on his knee and Jordan. They are three of his six Great Grandchildren.
*Courtesy of DC Thomson & Co Ltd, Dundee*

Society to a packed audience who brought the roof down as the artist mounted the stage to receive a framed copy of the score. A year earlier, in 1992, the famous Broons page in The Fun Section of "The Sunday Post" had featured the artist in one of its story lines involving his famous Tay Bridge painting, an accolade not to be taken lightly. Several university students have also chosen the work of McIntosh Patrick as the subject of dissertations in the history of art and some day, no doubt, there will be an in-depth examination of his life and work leading to a PhD degree.

There was one honour, however, which was the subject of much lobbying by the artist's friends and supporters, and that was the recognition they felt he deserved in the Queen's honours list. For nearly ten years prior to his death there was a steady, but very private, campaign to have him 'gonged' at royal level. These efforts, conducted without any family involvement whatsoever, were channelled through many corridors of power and influence. Letters of recommendation were submitted on a regular basis. There was also a personal appeal to John Major when he occupied 10 Downing Street. One leading business chief said he would pursue the cause through the Scottish Office, although warning that *the system is capricious and difficult to understand*. These overtures were all made before the nomination of honours was thrown open later to members of the public.

When the recognition finally came in 1997 in the form of an OBE for services to art, the artist, now 90, expressed delight but was unable to disguise his frustration and disappointment at being unable, on account of his failing health at that time, to attend the investiture at either Buckingham Palace or the Palace of Holyroodhouse in Edinburgh. In the event he was presented with his medal by Lord Provost Mervyn Rolfe, of Dundee, in his capacity as Lord Lieutenant of the city. The ceremony in the City Chambers was attended by three generations of the artist's family and proved to be a much more intimate occasion than he could have expected at an official investiture. But there is still a lingering feeling in certain circles that McIntosh Patrick, one of the finest and most popular landscape painters in Britain, outstanding teacher and supporter of charitable causes, should have been knighted at an earlier time.

There is one other honour which has to be mentioned. In December, 1978, the artist was nominated 'Dundee Citizen of the Year,' an honorary appointment made annually by a committee drawn from various sections of the community in recognition of work carried out for the benefit of others within the city. Receiving the trophy from Lord Provost Harry Vaughan the artist, with his usual sense of pawkiness, remarked: *I thought this honour usually went to someone who worked in charity, but I'm glad that someone thought there are other ways to give people pleasure without giving them soup.*

There was a feeling, however, then and since, that the City Council should have gone one stage further and given McIntosh Patrick the Freedom of Dundee, which is the highest honour a civic authority can award to an individual for outstanding public service. The Council has granted this distinction to ten people and one organisation (The Black Watch) since the end of the Second World War.

Throughout the years, at his exhibitions and on many other occasions, the artist and his work had been praised to the high heavens by various civic heads and councillors, his contribution to the cultural life of the city and his ambassadorial role far beyond it

*Everything has its beauty but not everyone sees it*

through his landscape painting, being generously acknowledged at the highest local level. *One of our most treasured sons* became a favoured tribute trotted out at countless civic functions.

If ever anyone had demonstrated with such abundance the qualities necessary for the Freedom, it was McIntosh Patrick, and although approaches had been made to grant him this honour the artist was never to be made a Freeman of the city he had given so much to throughout his working life.

Today McIntosh Patrick is remembered in the city of his birth through the name of a street (Patrick Place, near his former home), a function suite in a west end hotel, and a section of a local private art gallery which has also been named after him.

Following his death the City Council announced that a small exhibition of his work and personal mementoes would be staged in the Dundee City Art Gallery every January, with a McIntosh Patrick Award being competed for annually by sixth form pupils studying art at local authority schools. There was the hope, expressed privately, that The Shrubbery might be bought by the city, along with its contents, and maintained as a museum of his life and work. There was, however, no funding available for such a project, and so the proposition was always a non-starter.

But the reason why Dundee never conferred the Freedom of the City upon one of its finest citizens remains a mystery to this day.

# The Final Years

THROUGHOUT the 1980's and the first half of the 90's McIntosh Patrick - or *Mackie Pat* as many people affectionately called him - continued painting to a daily routine as unflinching to change as any imposed by the most conservative of occupations: walking his dog after breakfast; departing mid-morning with a packed lunch for his painting location; returning late afternoons, with possibly a bit of touching-up work in the studio in the evening if not involved in a public engagement. His energy and enthusiasm and adrenaline flow appeared to be undiminished by the passage of time. He cocked a snook at his pensioner status as he carried on riding the crest of a popularity wave sustained by exhibitions, burgeoning print sales, and public acclaim.

But he never lost the common touch and his infinite courtesy and old-world charm remained to the end, as did his insistence on always being formally dressed in jacket and tie. And although he may have exuded the air of a retired professor, painting was what he lived for. It was all he knew and everything continued to be subjugated to that need. Holidays, never a popular pastime, were now a thing of the past. He had rarely set foot outside Scotland since returning from the war and had certainly never used his passport again. His sole aim was to carry on at the easel for as long as he lived. As he was fond of saying: *There is no virtue in not working.*

Above: **Oil Seed Rape** *The Saddler Collection*

**Harvest Field Kinnordie**
*This late pencil sketch,*
*and the one on page 102*
*by permission of a private collector*

Harvest field
Kinnordie

This dream, however, was to fall a little short of realisation. In the end, despite diminishing eyesight caused by a detached retina which eventually closed down his right eye, it was the lack of energy through the ageing process which finally brought the curtain down on a career that had lasted almost seventy years spread over eight decades, and to many seemed set to defy the normal demands of mortality. He folded up his easel and closed the lid of his paint box for the last time in the spring of 1996 at the age of 89, two years before he died, and only shortly after he had retired from his teaching role. His easel would no longer be seen in the field.

But McIntosh Patrick wasn't quite finished even yet. Although now unable to stand and paint and concentrate on landscape compositions he could still sit and draw at home and that was what he now did, reverting to his basic skills of draughtmanship. In this final flush of activity he spent hours every day painstakingly drawing remarques, small pencil sketches on the bottom white border of his colour reproductions. These would be of various pastoral scenes unconnected to the subject of the print. He also produced larger drawings, usually copies of his original paintings, some with tints, which were sold as separate entities and found a ready market. One got the feeling that he could have scribbled a few lines on a sheet of paper and still found a buyer, such was his reputation.

This work continued despite a hip replacement at ninety which reduced his mobility to the capacity of a zimmer and a wheelchair. Then, eventually, the drawing, too, came to an end although, almost to the day he died, he continued to sign prints of his paintings, great piles of them which arrived at The Shrubbery in a never-ending flow of parcels. Since the death of his wife, Janet, in 1983, McIntosh Patrick had been looked after by a series of dedicated housekeepers and it was these women, in the final stages of his life and using a desk specially adapted to the artist's restricted movements, who helped him negotiate this conveyer belt system of churning out personally-signed reproductions. In doing this he was simply keeping faith with members of the public who appreciated a personal signature on one of his prints.

In these last days he could look back on a life of remarkable achievement, a career which produced a staggering output of approximately 2,500 paintings, etchings, and drawings. Apart from the artistic merit of everything he has done, his paintings form an important social history, recording the farming scene as it was before the mechanisation of the agricultural industry. He himself had mourned the disappearance of the stook and other features of labour-intensive farming. As for the demise of the horse, he often quoted the ploughman who had told him that working with a tractor might be quicker, but was an awful lot lonelier. *Ye canna hae much o' a blether wi' a machine*, he said. As McIntosh Patrick also once observed with much wistfulness: *I do not believe farm workers today can be called anything else but engineers.*

The end finally came on Tuesday, April 7, 1998, in his ninety-second year. To bird song in his beloved garden on a lovely spring evening, the Great Scot slipped away peacefully at home.

TRIBUTES to Scotland's most popular landscape painter of the 20th century bore the same stamp of sincerity and appreciation as the artist had himself always expressed for his subjects in everything he had drawn, etched, and painted. Newspaper coverage of his death, both locally and nationally, covered many column inches with journalists according him a fond farewell. Fleet Street played its part in all this testimony to a memorable career with the Scottish press disproving the theory that a Scot is only truly appreciated at home when he or she has staked their claim to fame in a foreign part. Here is a selection of quotes from the obituary coverage:

> James McIntosh Patrick was regarded as the most popular Scottish landscape artist of the 20th century and hailed by his peers as the most brilliant etcher of his age....*The Scotsman*.
> Patrick used perspective with all the verve and the curiosity of a hiker or an explorer, bringing many aspects of a scene together through his skills in design....*The Times*.

It is through his depiction of vistas around, and in, Dundee that many people who have never set foot in Scotland feel familiar with scenery in Angus, the Carse of Gowrie and the west end of the city. That is a formidable achievement....*Dundee Courier*.

He turned to oil painting and quickly established a new reputation as a landscapist of outstanding power and perception....*The Independent*.

Internationally recognised for his landscapes and scenes of his beloved home city, Dr Patrick was a 'weel-kent' figure to every Scot....*The Express*.

Originals and limited editions of his works hang in drawing rooms and offices all over the country....*The Herald*.

THE funeral service was held on Wednesday, April 15, in Dundee Parish Church (St.Mary's), known as the *City Church* and the one used for most civic occasions of a religious nature. The congregation, which included the Lord Provost, gathered from many parts to pay their last respects to the 'People's Artist,' led by the Rev Keith E. Hall, the minister at St. Mary's, and the Very Rev Dr James L. Weatherhead, former Moderator, and retired Principal Clerk, to the General Assembly of the Church of Scotland. Dr Weatherhead, a friend of the Patrick family and a Dundonian himself, paid the following tribute:

*A McIntosh Patrick watercolour of Gruinard Bay hung in the sitting room of the home in which I grew up, in the 1930's and 40's. I knew that the artist's friendship with my mother had begun in childhood, and she often spoke of her early memories of him, and of his tendency to fill any available surface with pencil drawings.*

*My first memory of him was when he was a guest of my parents, soon after I had acquired a flute. He took up the instrument and immediately played a few phrases on it, to let me hear how a flute should sound. He and my father were members of a body called the Symposium - a group of men*

**The Very Rev.
James L. Weatherhead**

who met regularly, taking turns to deliver papers, which were followed by discussion, to which no-one here will be surprised to learn that his contributions on any subject were as prolific as they were erudite.

My mother-in-law regularly made the journey from Kirriemuir to enjoy his Saturday morning classes, and also became a friend. It is thus a personal privilege for me now to be sharing in this service, in which we gratefully remember this talented, versatile, lively, and friendly man, of whom Lord Macfarlane has spoken so eloquently.

In the book which was published at the time of the exhibition to celebrate his 80th birthday, Roger Billcliffe says that some of his paintings are really portraits of trees, and continues, 'He believes he is almost mystic about trees and plant life, saying that he feels he should apologise to the grasses and plants that he damages as he sets up his easel in the corner of a field.'

I recall a television programme, made by the BBC's Religious Broadcasting Department, in which McIntosh Patrick, in similar vein, said that he spoke to the trees in his garden. Roger Billcliffe also writes of the artist's preference for man-made rather than God-made landscape - of his vision of a Scottish landscape which celebrates the role of man in its creation - and points out that his response to "nature in the raw" on the West coast of Scotland was not as sympathetic as it was to the cultivated hills of the east.

I find in this attitude a remarkable affinity with the teaching of the Bible about the stewardship of creation which God has entrusted to humankind. What passes often as nature in the raw in the Highlands is in fact the result of human sinfulness in the notorious clearances; and our current ecological concern about such things as the destruction of tropical rain-forests is also about the human sinfulness of exploitation rather than cultivation of nature.

Therefore, if McIntosh Patrick landscapes celebrate the role of man, that role as depicted in these paintings is precisely what the Bible teaches that it ought to be. Perhaps there is no better text for all this than the verse in Psalm 96: 'Let the field be joyful, and all that is therein; then shall all the trees of the wood rejoice.' I do regret that the artist whose work so vividly illustrates that text was not an active churchman. He could have been a very stimulating speaker in the General Assembly!

But I believe it to be a function of the Church to celebrate goodness, and quality, and integrity, wherever these are to be found, without asking legalistic questions about the ecclesiastical status of those responsible for such virtue. After all, the essence of the Gospel the Church has to proclaim is the grace, the unconditional love of God, which does not depend on our being on any membership list, or our subscribing to orthodox doctrines, or our moral rectitude, or our good works.

It was in love that God created the world, and in this Easter season we celebrate the conquest of death by that love, in Jesus Christ. Therefore, we are set free to give thanks to God without reservation for an artist of genius and integrity, a great man, a unique character, and a good friend - James McIntosh Patrick.

Dr Weatherhead then led the congregation in the prayer that followed:

Almighty God, Creator of the world, Author of life, and giver of victory, we thank You that in love You gave your Son, Jesus Christ, to live for us, to die for us, to conquer death for us, and to open to us the gate of eternal life. We thank You for the great company of those who, having died to us, are living with You, and for those among them whom we have known and loved, remembering especially today James McIntosh Patrick.

We praise You for his artistic talents, and the enthusiasm and dedication with which he used and developed them, to become an artist of immense significance, and to enhance the quality of life of so many who enjoyed his work. We thank

*You for the many honours he received: from the Queen, from this city and its universities, and from the Royal Academy of Scotland, and for the esteem in which he was so widely held.*

*We bless You for his many other talents, in teaching and speaking and music, in stimulating and encouraging, and in friendship. We remember also with gratitude the love he gave and received in his marriage, and in his family, and the help and care and companionship so freely given to him by others in his later years and times of infirmity.*

*As together we rejoice in the memories of him whom we hold dear, we give thanks for those most precious and tender memories which will ever be cherished by those closest to him in kinship and in love and affection, and we pray that You will sustain them in this time of pride and sadness. Grant that he may be to all of us an example of using talents to the full, of zest for living, and of interest in fellow men and women. O Lord, support us all the day long of this life, until the shadows lengthen and the evening comes, and the busy world is hushed, the fever of life is over, and our work done.*

*Then Lord, in your mercy, grant us safe lodging, a holy rest, and peace at the last; through Jesus Christ our Lord (there then followed the Lord's Prayer).*

A further tribute was paid by the artist's long-time friend and admirer, The Rt.Hon. Lord Macfarlane, of Bearsden, who recalled how McIntosh Patrick had endeared himself to his fellow citizens in Dundee, both by his artistic talent and his active participation in the life of the city. He added:

**The Rt Hon
Lord Macfarlane of Bearsden**

*I admired Jimmy Patrick for his integrity, his honesty in the application of his skill, his single-mindedness of purpose and above all, as a professional who lived for his work and was prepared to be judged by his efforts. He remained faithful to his own beliefs and principles, did not seek popularity at the expense of his art, and did not follow the trends, of which he was aware, if it meant being disloyal to his own standards. He was one of the most accomplished painters of his generation, who has won a special place in the artistic Hall of Fame through his talent and vision, but perhaps most of all his hard work.*

*Clara Young who organised the great 1987 retrospective exhibition of Jimmy Patrick's work said in the catalogue, at a time which was pretty fraught for both of them: 'Thanks to McIntosh Patrick for his unfailing charm, cheerful patience, enthusiastic encouragement, and also for just being his delightful self'. And one of his fellow Great Scots, Robert Louis Stevenson could have been speaking about Jimmy when he said: 'That man is a success, who has lived well, laughed often and loved much: who has gained the respect of intelligent men and the love of children: who has filled his niche and accomplished his task: who leaves the world better than he found it, whether by an improved poppy, a perfect poem, or a rescued soul: who never lacked appreciation of earth's beauty or failed to express it: who looked for the best in others and gave the best he had'*

*James McIntosh Patrick throughout his life certainly gave the best he had and we are all the better for it.*

The hymns were No 360 (Praise, my soul, the King of Heaven); No 154 (All things bright and beautiful); No 451 (Almighty Father of all things that be), which contained the deeply significant couplet:

> The grace of poet's pen or painter's hand
> to teach the loveliness of sea and land.

Following the service a reception was held in the appropriate setting of the spectacular Albert Hall in the city's art galleries, which had so often been a place of pilgrimage for those who admired the work of James McIntosh Patrick. Later there was a private cremation after which the ashes of the artist were scattered in the Carse of Gowrie. He had gone back to the landscape he loved most of all. There is, therefore, no headstone with a ringing epitaph by which to remember him. But asked once how he would like to be remembered he replied: *Oh, as a landscape painter, a Nature lover - someone who got great satisfaction out of the bit of the world he was born into and never found anything better.*